The
Least
You
Should
Know
about
Vocabulary
Building

Fourth Edition

The Least You Should Know about Vocabulary Building

Word Roots

TERESA FERSTER GLAZIER

Harcourt Brace Jovanovich College Publishers

Fort Worth   Philadelphia   San Diego   New York   Orlando   Austin
San Antonio   Toronto   Montreal   London   Sydney   Tokyo

Publisher	Ted Buchholz
Acquisitions Editor	Michael Rosenberg
Developmental Editor	Stacy Schoolfield
Senior Project Editor	Steve Welch
Production Manager	Cynthia Young
Book Designer	Beverly Baker

Address Editorial Correspondence To: Harcourt Brace Jovanovich, Inc.
301 Commerce Street, Suite 3700
Fort Worth, Texas 76102

Address Orders To: Harcourt Brace Jovanovich, Inc.
6277 Sea Harbor Drive
Orlando, Florida 32887
1-800-782-4479, or
1-800-433-0001 (in Florida)

Printed in the United States of America

ISBN: 0-15-500220-1

5 6 7 8 9 0 1   016   9 8 7 6 5 4

To the Instructor

Because learning to break words into their parts is perhaps the most important initial step in vocabulary building, this text helps students take that step and begin what should become an ongoing study of words. Whether the text is used in the classroom or for self-help, the following features make it easy to use with little guidance.

1. Since only one approach is used—word roots—students can work through the text easily. They learn a method of study while learning the first root and follow it throughout the book.
2. No distinction is made between Greek and Latin roots. Students need to remember the meaning of a root rather than its language source. Similarly, no distinction is made among roots, prefixes, and suffixes because all are equally sources of word meaning.
3. Students learn words in context. After a word is defined, it is then used in a sentence.
4. Some difficult words are included for those who happen to be ready for them, but students should be encouraged to concentrate on words they have encountered before and are curious about.
5. The simplest pronunciation aids are used, the only diacritical mark being the one for long vowels.
6. Answers at the back of the book allow students to teach themselves.
7. Three exercises with no answers provided (pp. 77, 117, 137) may be used as tests.
8. A Word Index simplifies using the text.

A packet of ready-to-photocopy tests is available to instructors upon adoption of the text and may be obtained from the local representative or from the English Editor, Harcourt Brace Jovanovich College Publishers, 301 Commerce Street, Suite 3700, Fort Worth, Texas 76102.

TFG

Acknowledgments

The idea for this book I owe to my father from whom I learned the meaning of such words as *propensity, convivial,* and *commodious* before I could read. I can still hear the creak of the old metal dictionary stand as my father would open the *Funk and Wagnalls New Standard Dictionary* to look up a word and then try the word out again and again on my mother and me. From him I learned to keep word lists and to probe for root meanings. This is really his book.

More recently I am indebted to my son Kenneth for exceptionally careful proofreading.

Contents

Increasing Your Vocabulary through Learning Word Roots

How did words get to be words? Why, for example, is a hippopotamus called a hippopotamus and not a glipserticka? There's a good reason. Since the animal looks a bit like a fat horse and spends much of its time in rivers, the Greeks combined their word for horse, HIPPOS, and their word for river, POTAMOS, and called the animal a hippopotamos, a river horse. And with only a one-letter change, the word has come down to us as hippopotamus.

Words did not just happen. They grew. And if you learn how they grew—what original roots they came from—you'll find it easier to remember them. You'll *understand* the words you look up in the dictionary instead of just memorizing the definitions. And weeks later, even though you may have forgotten the meaning of a word, your knowledge of its roots[1] will help you recall its meaning.

The best first step in vocabulary building, then, is to become familiar with some word roots because learning the root of one word often gives a clue to dozens or hundreds more. For example, if you learn that SYN (SYM, SYL) means *together* or *with*, you have a clue to more than 450 words, for that many words beginning with SYN (SYM, SYL) are listed in *Webster's Third New International Dictionary*. Similarly, when you learn that *philanthropist* is made up of PHIL to *love* and ANTHROP *human*, you have learned not only that a philanthropist is a lover of humanity, but you also have a clue to some 70 other words beginning with PHIL and to more than 60 others beginning with ANTHROP, not to mention those that have PHIL or ANTHROP in the middle or at the end of the word.

As you become aware of how words are made up, familiar words will take on new meaning, and unfamiliar words may often be understood even without a dictionary. For instance, if you know that the root BIBL means *book* as in *bibliography* and *Bible*, then you can guess that a *bibliophile* will have something to do with books. And if you remember that PHIL means to *love*, as in *philanthropist* (lover of humanity), then you will immediately guess that a bibliophile must be a lover of books.

---

[1]In this book the term roots includes prefixes and suffixes because all word parts are equally sources of word meaning. All are the roots from which our language came.

Glancing at the root chain below will help you spot some common roots. The chain begins with *biped* [BI two + PED foot], a two-footed animal. The next word contains one of the preceding roots, PED. A *pedometer* [PED foot + METER measure] is, as its roots indicate, a "foot measure" or an instrument that measures the distance walked by recording the number of steps taken. The next word must contain METER, and out of the hundreds of METER words, *geometry* [GEO earth + METER measure] has been chosen. As its roots show, geometry was originally a system of "earth measuring," that is, of measuring the earth through the use of angles. The next word must contain GEO, and so on.

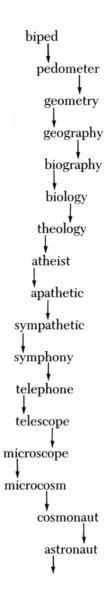

biped

pedometer

geometry

geography

biography

biology

theology

atheist

apathetic

sympathetic

symphony

telephone

telescope

microscope

microcosm

cosmonaut

astronaut

astronomy

↓

autonomy

↓

automobile

↓

immobile

↓

infidel

↓

confident

↓

committee

↓

transmit

↓

transport

↓

report

↓

recur

↓

excursion

↓

exclude

↓

seclude

↓

secure

↓

manicure

↓

manuscript

↓

subscribe

↓

subversive

↓

controversy

↓

contradict

↓

benediction

↓

benefactor

↓

facilitate

This root chain ends with *facilitate* (to make easier). Perhaps reading the chain will facilitate your spotting word roots in the future.

After you've learned some of the roots in this book, try to make a root chain of your own.

Learning word roots is not only the quickest way to increase your vocabulary but also the most entertaining. For example, did you know . . .

that **salary** [SAL salt] originally was the money paid to Roman soldiers to buy salt . . .

that a **companion** [COM with + PAN bread] was originally a person one shared one's bread with . . .

that **malaria** [MAL bad + AER air] was so named because people thought it was caused by the bad air of the swamps . . .

that a **terrier** [TERR earth] got its name because it digs in the earth after small animals in burrows . . .

that **escape** [ES out + CAP cape] originally meant to get out of one's cape, leaving it in the hands of the pursuer . . .

that an **insect** [IN in + SECT to cut] was so named because its body is "cut" into three segments . . .

that a **bonfire** in the Middle Ages was the bone fire built to dispose of corpses during the plague . . .

that **panic** originally described the frantic efforts of the Greek nymphs to escape when the mischievous god Pan suddenly appeared among them . . .

that **curfew** in the Middle Ages in France was the ringing of a bell telling the peasants to cover their fires *(couvre-feu)* for the night . . .

that **alphabet** comes from the first two letters of the Greek alphabet, ALPHA and BETA, "a" and "b" . . .

that **trivia** [TRI three + VIA way] in Roman times meant the crossroads where three ways met and where neighborhood gossips on their way to market often stopped to chat about unimportant things (TRI VIA talk) . . .

that **preposterous** [PRE before + POST after] originally meant having the before part where the after part should be, like a horse with its tail where its head should be—in other words, absurd.

As you look up words in your dictionary, you may uncover other interesting stories if you note the word roots, which will be found in square brackets either just before or just after the definition.

Where to Find Word
Roots in Your Dictionary

Most dictionaries give the derivation (word roots) of words. You'll find the derivation either just after or just before the definition.

The American Heritage Dictionary, Second College Edition[1]

> **eu·pho·ny** (yōō'fə-nē) *n., pl.* **-nies**. Agreeable sound. esp. in the phonetic quality of words. [Fr. *euphonie* < LLat. *euphonia* < Gk. < *euphōnos*, sweet-voiced : *eu-*, good + *phōnē*, sound.]

The derivation is in square brackets at the end of the definition. The last part of the derivation gives the original roots: *eu-*, good + *phone*, sound.

Webster's New World Dictionary[2]

> **eu·pho·ny** (-nē) *n., pl.* **-nies** [Fr. *euphonie* < LL. *euphonia* < Gr. *euphōnia* < *euphōnos*, sweet-voiced, musical < *eu-*, well + *phōnē*, voice: see PHONE[1]] the quality of having a pleasing sound; pleasant combination of agreeable sounds in spoken words; also, such a combination of words

The derivation is in square brackets before the definition. The last part of the derivation gives the original roots: *eu-*, well + *phone*, voice.

Webster's Ninth New Collegiate Dictionary[3]

> **eu·pho·ny** \'yü-fə-nē\ *n, pl* **-nies** [F *euphonie*, fr. LL *euphonia*, fr. Gk *euphōnia*, fr. *euphōnos* sweet-voiced, musical, fr. *eu-* + *phōnē* voice — more at BAN] (ca. 1623) **1** : pleasing or sweet sound; *esp* : the acoustic effect produced by words so formed or combined as to please the ear   **2** : a harmonious succession of words having a pleasing sound —

The derivation is in square brackets before the definition. The last part of the derivation gives the original roots and the meaning of one of them: *phone*, voice. To find the meaning of the other root, look for *eu-* as a regular dictionary entry. There its meaning is given: well or good.

Thus the roots indicate that *euphony* means good sound or good voice. And when you look at the definitions, you'll find that that is exactly what it means: agreeable sound; the quality of having a pleasing sound; pleasing or sweet sound. Having learned the roots of *euphony*, you'll remember the word longer than if you had merely looked up the definition.

[1] Copyright © 1985 by Houghton Mifflin Company. Reprinted by permission.
[2] © 1988. Used by permission of the publisher, New World Dictionaries/A division of Simon & Schuster, New York.
[3] By permission. From *Webster's Ninth New Collegiate Dictionary* © 1991 by Merriam-Webster Inc., publisher of the Merriam-Webster® dictionaries.

Changes in Root Spelling

A root may change its spelling slightly according to the word it is in. For example, EX *out* is found in **excursion,** but it changes to ES in **escape** and to simply E in **educate**. Such changes have occurred to make pronunciation easier. Escape and educate are easier to pronounce than excape and exducate would be. Here are some of the ways root spellings change.

Sometimes the last letter of a root changes to be like the first letter of the root that follows:

COM nect	becomes	CON nect
COM loquial	becomes	COL loquial
COM relate	becomes	COR relate
DIS fident	becomes	DIF fident
SYN metrical	becomes	SYM metrical

Sometimes the last letter of a root changes (or is dropped) to make the pronunciation easier, but it doesn't become the same as the first letter of the root that follows:

EX cape	becomes	ES cape
COM temporary	becomes	CON temporary
SYN pathy	becomes	SYM pathy
DIS vert	becomes	DI vert
EX ducate	becomes	E ducate

A root may also appear in slightly different forms in different words. CLUD, *to close, to shut,* may appear as

CLUD	in	seclude
CLUS	in	recluse
CLAUS	in	claustrophobia
CLOS	in	closet

but you'll soon learn to spot a root even when its spelling varies.

How to Use This Book

It makes little difference which root you study first because each root will help you eventually with some new word. Therefore the roots in this text are presented alphabetically.

Don't worry if on a page you find a few words you're not acquainted with. They're included merely for anyone who happens to be ready for them. Concentrate on words you've heard or seen before and wondered about, words you almost know but aren't quite sure of. They're the ones you can learn most easily. And mastering even a few words under each root will give quite a boost to your vocabulary.

Here are six steps to take as you begin your study.

1. First, take the PRELIMINARY TEST on page 9. At the end of your study you'll have a chance to take a similar test to see how the study of word roots has increased your vocabulary.
2. Now turn to the first root—A, AN on page 12.
   (For help with pronunciation see the **Pronunciation Key** on the inside front cover of this book.)
   Note that not every root of every word is explained but only those that will help you remember the word.
   The first definition is often a literal one (marked *lit.*) taken directly from the meaning of the roots. The definitions that follow are current ones.
3. After you have studied all the words on the page, then do Exercise 1 and correct your answers by those in the Answer section beginning on page 139.
4. Study again any words you missed—if they are ones you want to add to your vocabulary.
5. Next use some of the words in your own writing. Begin to keep a vocabulary journal, writing each day two or three sentences about whatever interests you and using some of the words you have just learned. Putting the words into your own writing will help you remember them longer than if you merely fill in blanks. And from time to time you can reread your journal to review your words.
6. Finally, take the most important step in vocabulary building—use your newly learned words in conversation. Using a word in conversation will do more to help you remember it than any amount of silent study. USE A WORD THREE TIMES AND IT'S YOURS. Try using one

new word a day. Begin at breakfast, and during the day find two more opportunities to use the word. Once you have used it three times, you'll be surprised how easily it will slip into your conversation. And even if it's a word you don't expect to use, it will stay in your passive vocabulary so that you'll recognize it when you encounter it in your reading.

PRELIMINARY TEST   Test yourself on these words taken from college textbooks and current magazines. Check your answers with those on page 139.

_____ 1. ambiguous   A. very large   B. having two possible meanings
C. seeking fame   D. exceptionally clear

_____ 2. philanthropic   A. unmoved by criticism   B. fond of animals
C. sociable   D. charitable

_____ 3. antipathy   A. strong dislike   B. worry   C. kindly feelings
D. ancient times

_____ 4. autonomous   A. self-governing   B. governed by a few
C. governed by a dictator   D. without any government

_____ 5. benefactor   A. one who receives money from a will   B. one who
receives a grant   C. distant relative   D. one who gives assistance

_____ 6. anachronism   A. mistake in grammar   B. something out of its proper
historical time   C. incorrect calculation   D. clock for navigation

_____ 7. circumscribe   A. to overcome circumstances   B. to write an
autograph   C. to restrict the action of   D. to denounce

_____ 8. convivial   A. sociable   B. superficial   C. dangerous to life   D. vivid

_____ 9. credulous A.   unbelieving   B. believing too readily   C. suspicious
D. having a good credit rating

_____ 10. precursor   A. supervisor   B. beginner   C. forerunner   D. financial
officer

_____ 11. pandemic   A. causing illness   B. causing a wild uproar
C. undemocratic   D. widespread

_____ 12. euphemism   A. substitution of a pleasant for an unpleasant word
B. substitution of a specific term for a general one   C. false
statement   D. unrestrained praise

_____ 13. enervate   A. to weaken   B. to strengthen   C. to soothe   D. to excite

_____ 14. epilogue   A. speech at a funeral   B. speech at the end of a play
C. speech at the beginning of a play   D. speech of apology

_____ 15. loquacious   A. full of life   B. having the ability to see through things
C. understanding several languages   D. talkative

_____ 16. malinger   A. move slowly   B. spend too much time on details
C. pretend to be ill to get out of work   D. waste time

_____ 17. missive   A. lost article   B. missing part   C. wrong answer   D. letter

_____ 18. metamorphosis   A. life of a butterfly   B. change of form   C. mental illness   D. abnormal growth

_____ 19. panacea   A. remedy for all ills   B. folk remedy   C. widespread epidemic   D. view from a mountain

_____ 20. apathy   A. dislike   B. strong interest   C. indifference   D. sympathy

_____ 21. impediment   A. lack of funds   B. hindrance   C. inability to speak   D. inability to walk

_____ 22. progeny   A. plan of action   B. gifted child   C. descendants   D. ancestors

_____ 23. assiduous   A. overbearing   B. haughty   C. critical   D. persevering

_____ 24. auspicious   A. unfavorable   B. favorable   C. foreboding evil   D. having doubts

_____ 25. subterranean   A. under cover   B. under the ocean   C. under the earth   D. underhanded

_____ 26. supercilious   A. haughty   B. socially prominent   C. intellectually superior   D. solicitous

_____ 27. syndrome   A. place where horse races are held   B. stadium   C. two adjoining domes   D. symptoms occurring together

WORD ROOTS IN ALPHABETICAL ORDER

A, AN—not, without

When A or AN meaning *not* or *without* comes at the beginning of certain words, it gives those words a negative meaning. Anything that is **asymmetrical** is *not* symmetrical, and anything that is **atypical** is *not* typical.

Atheist and **agnostic** both begin with the negative A and are close in meaning. An atheist [A without + THE god] is *without* a God whereas an agnostic [A not + GNOS to know] does *not* know whether there is a God. In other words, the atheist is sure there is no God whereas the agnostic simply does not know.

Note how A or AN gives each of the following words a negative meaning.

agnostic (ag nos' tik) [A not + GNOS to know]—one who does not know whether there is a God. *He had lost his former faith and had become an agnostic.*

amoral (ā mawr' ul)—*lit.* without moral standards; neither moral nor immoral; unable to distinguish between right and wrong. *Infants are amoral.*

anarchy (an' ur kē) [AN without + ARCH ruler]—*lit.* without a ruler; political disorder and confusion. *The overthrow of the government resulted in anarchy.*

anecdote (an' ik dōt) [AN not + EKDOTOS given out]—originally, not published (some stories were made public by publishing them, and others were kept private); now, merely a short account of some interesting or humorous incident. *The speaker enlivened his talk with humorous anecdotes.*

anemia (uh nē' mē uh) [AN without + HEM blood]—*lit.* without blood; a deficiency of red corpuscles in the blood. *Her weakness was caused by anemia.*

anesthetic (an is thet' ik) [AN without + ESTHET feeling]—*lit.* without feeling; a drug causing one to be insensitive to pain. *Before the operation he was given an anesthetic.*

anomaly (uh nom' uh lē) [AN not + HOMO same]—*lit.* not the same (as others); a rare exception; something that is not normal. *Charles Darwin wrote, "There is no greater anomaly in nature than a bird that cannot fly."*

anonymous (uh non' uh mus) [AN without + ONYM name]—*lit.* without a name; having an unknown or unacknowledged name. *The donor of the new building wished to remain anonymous.*

asymmetrical (ā si met' ri kul) or **asymmetric** [A not + SYM together + METER measure]—*lit.* not measured together; not having both sides exactly alike; not symmetrical. *She preferred asymmetrical flower arrangements.*

atheist (ā′ thē ist) [A without + THE god]—*lit.* one who is without a God; one who denies the existence of God. *As an atheist, she objected to the nativity scene in the town square at Christmas.*

atypical (ā tip′ i kul)—not typical. *A classical concert performed by a rock group would certainly be atypical.*

ALSO: amorphous, analgesic, apathetic, apathy, atom. (Look in the Word Index on page 149 for these words. Some are discussed under their other roots.)

☐**EXERCISE 1** Write the appropriate A, AN word. Answers to the exercises will be found at the back of the book beginning on page 139.

1. In her autobiography the author includes many interesting _____ from her childhood.
2. The flower arrangement was _____, with one side taller than the other.
3. The person who donated the new library building didn't want recognition; he

    wished to remain _____.

4. My cat is an _____; it doesn't like to chase birds.

5. The small nation was in a state of _____ after the overthrow of the government.
6. She had always been an _____, not knowing whether there is a God.
7. Finally she became an _____, denying the existence of God.
8. When the suspect in the murder trial was found to be totally lacking in moral

    standards, the judge labeled her _____.

9. Before the discovery of _____, people were sometimes made unconscious before an operation by a blow on the head.
10. Either decreased production or increased destruction of red blood cells may

    cause _____.
11. My friend is usually so gracious that her leaving without even saying thank you

    was _____.

☐**EXERCISE 2** The best way to remember new words is to use them immediately in your writing and speaking. Therefore begin a vocabulary journal in which you write daily two or three sentences using some of your new words. If you write about things that interest you, then you'll be inclined to reread your journal occasionally as a review.

AMBI, AMPHI—around, both

In Roman times, candidates for public office, wearing white togas so that they could be easily seen, walked *around* (AMBI) talking to people and seeking votes. Before long, the term *ambitio* took on the meaning of bribery in seeking votes, but by the time the word came into English in the fourteenth century as **ambitious,** it had lost the idea of seeking votes or of bribery and meant merely "eager to succeed or to advance."

ambience (am' bē uns) [AMBI around]—the surrounding atmosphere. *The long pictures on the walls and the paper lanterns gave the restaurant an oriental ambience.*

ambiguous (am big' yoo us) [AMBI around + AGERE to drive]—*lit.* to drive around (in an uncertain manner because there were few roads in early days); uncertain; having two possible meanings. *From her ambiguous answer, I couldn't tell whether she was complimenting or insulting me.*

ambitious (am bish' us)—originally, going around for votes; today, having a desire to succeed. *She's ambitious and hopes to get a better job.*

amphitheater (am fuh thē' uh tur)—an oval or round structure with tiers of seats around an open space. *The Drama Department presented* Peer Gynt *in the university amphitheater.*

In the preceding words AMBI or AMPHI means *around*. In the following words it means *both*.

ambidextrous (am bi dek' strus) [AMBI both + DEXTR right hand]—*lit.* both right hands; able to use both hands with equal ease. *Because she is ambidextrous, she plays a great game of tennis.*

ambiguity (am bi gyoo' uh tē) [AMBI both]—the quality of having two possible meanings. *The ambiguity in his writing leaves the reader puzzled.*

ambivalence (am biv' uh luns)—conflicting (both kinds of) feelings toward a person or thing. *The boy was experiencing ambivalence about giving his speech, wanting to give it and yet dreading it.*

ambivalent (am biv' uh lunt)—having conflicting (both kinds of) feelings toward someone or something. *A child often feels ambivalent about a new baby in the family, both liking it and resenting it.*

amphibian (am fib' ē un) [AMPHI both + BIO life]—an animal that lives both in the water and on land. *Frogs, toads, and salamanders are amphibians.* Also, an aircraft that can take off and land both on water and on land.

amphibious (am fib' ē us) [AMPHI both + BIO life]—able to live or to travel both on land and in water. *The Marines went ashore in amphibious vehicles.*

☐**EXERCISE 1** Match each word with its definition.

A. ambidextrous   C. amphitheater   E. ambivalent
B. amphibian   D. ambiguous   F. ambience

_____ 1. able to use both hands with equal ease

_____ 2. an open structure with tiers of seats around an open space

_____ 3. an animal that lives both in the water and on land

_____ 4. the surrounding atmosphere

_____ 5. having conflicting feelings toward someone or something

_____ 6. having two possible meanings

☐**EXERCISE 2** Write the appropriate AMBI, AMPHI word.

1. The senator's _____ statements made me unsure of how he would vote on the issue.

2. She felt _____ toward her baby brother, both loving him and hating him.

3. His _____ toward the army made him undecided about reenlisting.

4. The spicy aroma of Mideastern cuisine and the bright tapestries gave the restaurant an exotic _____.

5. The _____ of that statement leaves it open to several interpretations.

6. Our class is going to the lake to study frogs and other _____.

7. My brother can bat and pitch with either hand because he's _____.

8. Every seat in the _____ was filled for the Commencement Exercises.

Answers to the exercises will be found at the back of the book beginning on page 139.

☐**EXERCISE 3** Write three sentences in your vocabulary journal using some of the AMBI, AMPHI words you have learned. Check with the sentence given in the explanation of each word to make sure you are using the word correctly. For example, *ambiguous* is an adjective whereas *ambiguity* is a noun. But even without thinking about parts of speech, you'll use the words correctly if you follow the model sentences.

ANN, ENN—year

Words containing ANN or ENN will have something to do with *year*. An **anniversary** is the return of some event every *year*. An **annuity** is a fund that pays a person money every *year*. **Annual** means happening every *year*, and **semiannual** means happening every half *year*. **Biannual** and **biennial** are easily confused because they both come from BI *two* and ANN or ENN *year*. Just remember that **biannual** and **semiannual** (both meaning twice a year) sound alike whereas **biennial** (meaning every two years) sounds different.

annals (an' uls) [ANN year]—a written account of events year by year; historical records. *We searched the annals of the medical society to find when the vaccine had first been tested.*

anniversary (an uh vurs' uh rē) [ANN year + VERS to turn]—the yearly return of the date of some memorable event. *We're making plans for our parents' wedding anniversary.*

annual (an' yōō ul) [ANN year]—yearly. *We have an annual family reunion.* Also, lasting only one year, as an annual plant. *She liked annual plants even though she had to replace them every year.*

annuity (uh nōō' uh tē)—an investment that provides fixed payments yearly or at other regular intervals. *After paying into his annuity for years, he now receives a check every month.*

biannual (bī an' yōō ul) [BI two + ANN year]—occurring two times a year. *The treasurer made biannual (or semiannual) reports in January and July.*

biennial (bī en' ē ul) [BI two + ENN year]—occurring every two years. *The society holds a biennial convention in the odd-numbered years.*

centennial (sen ten' ē ul) [CENT hundred + ENN year]—a 100th anniversary. *The Exposition in Montreal in 1967 celebrated the centennial of Canadian Confederation.*

millennium (muh len' ē um) [MILLI thousand + ENN year]—a period of a thousand years; specifically, the thousand years when, according to the New Testament, Christ is to reign on earth; thus a period of happiness and prosperity. *Some reformers today are hoping for nothing short of a millennium.*

per annum (pur an' um) [PER through + ANN year]—by the year; annually. *The chairperson received a fixed salary per annum.*

perennial (puh ren' ē ul) [PER through + ENN year]—having a life cycle lasting through more than two years, as a perennial plant. *In his garden he planted only perennials so that he wouldn't have to replant every year.* Also, lasting many years, as perennial youth. *She was a perennial student, still taking courses after she was 50.*

semiannual (sem ē an' yōō ul) [SEMI half + ANN year]—half yearly; occurring two times a year. *He made semiannual reports in January and July.*

superannuated (soo pur an' yoo ā tid) [SUPER above + ANN year]—*lit.* beyond the year of retirement; retired because of age. *Now that he was superannuated, he had time for his hobbies.*

ALSO: Anno Domini (abbrev. A.D.), bicentennial, triennial

□**EXERCISE 1**   What word containing ANN or ENN names the following?

1. a 100th anniversary _____

2. a period of great happiness and prosperity _____

3. a written account of events year by year _____
4. an   investment   providing   payments   yearly   or   at   other   intervals

   _____

5. the yearly return of the date of a memorable event _____

What word containing ANN or ENN describes the following?

6. something happening twice a year _____ or _____

7. something happening every two years _____

8. something lasting through many years _____

9. retired because of age _____

□**EXERCISE 2   REVIEW**   Fill in the blanks with words from the last three sections.
1. The vivid yellows and reds in the room created an _____ of warmth and vitality.
2. The lecturer did not make his point clear and left the audience puzzled by

   his _____.
3. I assure you that I don't usually miss appointments; my missing that one was

   definitely _____.

4. I'm feeling _____ about volunteering for that job. I know I should do it, but I really don't want to.

5. The ostrich is an _____; it's a bird, but it can't fly.

6. Luckily our plane was an _____ because we had to come down on the water.
7. I wrote my paper on toads and other _____.

ANTE, ANTI—before

The ANTE spelling always means *before*—either *before* in place or *before* in time. **Anteroom** and **anterior** are *before* in place whereas **ante, antedate,** and **antebellum** are *before* in time.

Another before-in-time word is **antediluvian**. Originally it meant *before the Flood* described in the Bible story of Noah and the Ark. In fact its two roots say exactly that [ANTE before + DILUVIUM flood], but today it has come to mean merely very old or primitive. Whenever you want to exaggerate the age of something, you can call it antediluvian. Young people may think their parents' ideas are antediluvian. A farmer without a tractor or a large office without a computer might be described as using antediluvian methods. And if you are trying to convince someone—or yourself—that your car is old enough to be traded in on a new model, you might refer to it as antediluvian.

ante (an' tē) [ANTE before]—the amount each poker player must put into the pot before receiving his cards. *Feeling confident, he upped the ante.*

antebellum (an ti bel' um) [ANTE before + BELL war]—before the war, especially before the Civil War. *The novel* Gone with the Wind *begins in the South in antebellum days.*

antecedent (an tuh sēd' unt) [ANTE before + CED to go]—anything that logically goes before something else. *Cricket was the antecedent of baseball.* Also, the word, phrase, or clause to which a pronoun refers. *In the sentence "Every boy was in his place,"* boy *is the antecedent of the pronoun* his.

antedate (an' ti dāt)—to occur before something else. *The Revolutionary War antedates the Civil War.*

antediluvian (an ti di lōō' vē un) [ANTE before + DILUVIUM flood]—before the Flood described in the Bible; old-fashioned or primitive. *Compared with the cars my friends drive, mine is antediluvian.*

ante meridiem (an ti muh rid' ē um) (abbreviated A.M.) [ANTE before + MERIDI noon]—before noon. *I have an appointment at 10 A.M.*

anterior (an tir' ē ur)—located before or in front (as opposed to posterior, located behind). *The anterior legs of the kangaroo are shorter than the posterior ones.*

anteroom (an' ti rōōm)—a room before the main room; a waiting room. *In the director's anteroom were a dozen actors waiting to try out for the part.*

A variant spelling—ANTI—also means before-in-time in the following words.

anticipate (an tis' uh pāt) [ANTI before + CAP to take]—*lit.* to take before; to realize beforehand. *No one anticipated such an outcome.*

antiquarian (an ti kwer' ē un)—one who collects or studies objects of former times. *The antiquarian appraised the rare first edition of Sandburg.*

antiquated (an' tuh kwā tid)—so old as to be no longer useful. *The factory had to replace the antiquated machinery.*

antique (an tēk')—belonging to an earlier (before) period. *In the parade were a dozen antique automobiles.*

antiquity (an tik' wuh tē)—ancient (before) times. *The museum specializes in armor from antiquity.*

(ANTI meaning *against* or *opposite* will be found on page 22.)

☐**EXERCISE 1**   Write the appropriate ANTE, ANTI word.

1. The office manager discarded some _____ typewriters.
2. She thought her parents' rules so hopelessly old-fashioned that she called

   them _____.
3. A grasshopper's wings are attached to the _____ part of its body.
4. Trees with hanging Spanish moss surrounded the old Southern mansion of

   the _____ period.

5. We found an _____ who was willing to buy the battered old copy of *Walden*.
6. In the museum were various artifacts from _____.

7. The landing of the Norsemen on this continent is said to _____ the landing of Columbus.
8. I dropped out of the poker game because the _____ was too high.
9. Not until this year did I learn that the _____ of a pronoun is the word it refers to.

10. No one had _____ that our team would win the tournament.

ANTHROP—human

Knowing that ANTHROP means *human* clarifies the meaning of a number of words. **Anthropology** [ANTHROP human + -LOGY study of] is a study of the development and behavior of *human* beings. A **philanthropist** [PHIL to love + ANTHROP human] loves *human* beings and promotes *human* welfare by charitable acts or gifts. A **misanthrope** [MIS to hate + ANTHROP human], on the other hand, hates *human* beings.

anthropoid (an' thruh poid) [ANTHROP human + OID resembling]— resembling humans. *Gorillas, chimpanzees, orangutans, and gibbons are anthropoid apes.*

anthropologist (an thruh pol' uh jist) [ANTHROP human + -LOGY study of]—one who studies the physical, social, and cultural development and behavior of human beings. *The anthropologist Margaret Mead lived for a time in Samoa to study the Samoan culture.*

anthropology (an thruh pol' uh jē) [ANTHROP human + -LOGY study of]—a study of the physical, social, and cultural development and behavior of human beings. *The anthropology professor commented that Eskimos have many words for snow.*

anthropomorphic (an thruh pō mawr' fik) [ANTHROP human + MORPH form]—thought of as having human form or characteristics. *The animal characters in Beatrix Potter's* Peter Rabbit *are anthropomorphic, speaking and acting like humans.*

anthropomorphism (an thruh pō mawr' fiz um) [ANTHROP human + MORPH form]—the attributing of human form or characteristics to a god, animal, or inanimate thing. *Anthropomorphism is a part of many primitive cultures, with rivers, trees, and animals being given human characteristics.*

misanthrope (mis' un thrōp) [MIS to hate + ANTHROP human]—one who hates people. *Only a misanthrope would have such a low opinion of the human race.*

misanthropic (mis un throp' ik) [MIS to hate + ANTHROP human]—characterized by hatred or scorn for people. *Ebenezer Scrooge shows his misanthropic attitude when he replies to a Merry Christmas greeting with "Bah! Humbug!"*

philanthropic (fil un throp' ik) [PHIL to love + ANTHROP human]—charitable. *The United Fund aids many philanthropic organizations.*

philanthropist (fi lan' thruh pist) [PHIL to love + ANTHROP human]—one who loves people, particularly one who gives money to benefit humanity. *Andrew Carnegie, a famous philanthropist, gave money to build public libraries.*

philanthropy (fil lan′ thruh pē) [PHIL to love + ANTHROP human]—the effort to increase the well-being of humanity by charitable donations. *The corporation was known for its philanthropy as well as for its good business practices.*

☐**EXERCISE 1**   Write the appropriate ANTHROP word.

1. The Uncle Remus stories about Br'er Rabbit have _____ characters.
2. I heard a lecture on the culture of the Amazon by a famous_____.
3. His hateful attitude toward his neighbors branded him as a_____.
4. Taking a course in _____ has given her a desire to travel to many countries.
5. Sign language can be taught to an _____ ape such as the chimpanzee.
6. The college is hoping that some _____ will donate a large sum to its endowment fund.

☐**EXERCISE 2**   List at least three stories or cartoons that have anthropomorphic characters.

☐**EXERCISE 3**   In your vocabulary journal write some sentences using ANTHROP words.

ANTI—against, opposite

ANTI meaning *against* is easy to spot in such words as **antifreeze, antitrust,** and **antisocial,** but it can also help clarify more difficult words.

A couple of ANTI words, which you probably won't have occasion to use and which won't be included in any of the tests in this book, are interesting just because of their stories.

Antipodes (an tip' uh dēz) [ANTI opposite + POD foot] means literally "with the feet opposite" and refers to any place on the *opposite* side of the earth since the people there seem to be standing upside down with their feet *opposite* to ours. The British refer to Australia and New Zealand as the Antipodes because those countries are on the *opposite* side of the earth.

Another word with an unusual history is **antimacassar** (an ti muh kas' ur). In the nineteenth century, men used macassar oil, imported from Macassar, Indonesia, as a hair dressing, and the oil often left grease spots on the back of upholstered chairs where the men rested their heads. Their wives, therefore, made small covers to put on the backs of the chairs to keep the macassar oil from soiling the upholstery. The covers were called antimacassars [ANTI against + MACASSAR macassar oil]. Gradually all covers protecting the backs and arms of upholstered furniture came to be called antimacassars.

antagonist (an tag' uh nist) [ANTI against + AGON struggle]—a person one struggles against in a contest. *The young wrestler was stronger than his antagonist.*

antibiotic (an ti bī ot' ik) [ANTI against + BIO life]—a substance produced by a microorganism that destroys other harmful (living) microorganisms. *Penicillin is an antibiotic.*

antidote (an' ti dōt) [ANTI against + DOT to give]—a medicine that counteracts (works against) poison or disease. *After the snake bit him, he was quickly given an antidote.* Also, something that gives protection against injurious effects. *Plentiful jobs are one of the best antidotes to crime.* Also, something that gives relief against something else. *The comedy was a pleasant antidote to all the tragedies we had seen.*

antiseptic (an tuh sep' tik) [ANTI against + SEPT putrid]—against infection; capable of destroying microorganisms that cause disease. *The nurse washed the wound with an antiseptic solution.*

In the preceding words ANTI means *against;* in the following words it means *opposite.*

Antarctica (ant ark′ ti kuh)—the continent opposite the Arctic. *The Arctic is the region at the North Pole; Antarctica is the continent opposite it at the South Pole.*

anticlimax (an ti klī′ maks)—*lit.* the opposite of the climax; a sudden drop from the important to the commonplace. *Her present uninteresting job is an anticlimax to a brilliant career.*

antithesis (an tith′ uh sis) [ANTI opposite + THES to place]—*lit.* one idea placed opposite another; the exact opposite. *Love is the antithesis of hate.* Also, ideas contrasted in balanced phrases, as *"To err is human; to forgive, divine."*

ALSO: antacid, antagonize, antipathy, antiphonal, antitoxin, antonym. (Look in the Word Index on page 149 for these words. Some are discussed under their other roots.)

□EXERCISE 1 Write the appropriate ANTI word.

1. Coming at the end of a stimulating program, his dull speech was an

   _____.
2. The man who challenged him to fight was a powerful _____.
3. He wanted luxury; she wanted a simple life. Thus his goals were the

   _____ of hers.
4. Diseases that were once fatal can now be cured with _____.

5. Having an interesting hobby is an _____ to boredom.

6. The continent of _____ surrounds the South Pole.

7. Modern _____ prevent open wounds from becoming infected.

□EXERCISE 2 REVIEW On one of the blank pages at the end of this book, start a WORD LIST of words you hope to use in the future. Keeping a word list is an excellent way to increase your vocabulary because rereading your list occasionally will bring to mind words you might otherwise forget.

AUTO—self

AUTO, meaning *self*, was a common Greek root, but it took on added meaning in America in the late nineteenth century when it was applied to the new vehicle that could "move by itself"—the automobile [AUTO self + MOB to move].

autocracy (aw tok' ruh sē) [AUTO self + CRAC to rule]—government by a single person. *The country had become an autocracy and was ripe for revolt.*

autocrat (aw' tuh krat) [AUTO self + CRAT to rule]—an absolute ruler; a domineering, self-willed person. *When the autocrat took over the country, the people lost all their power.*

autocratic (aw tuh krat' ik) [AUTO self + CRAT to rule]—*lit.* ruling by oneself; domineering. *The supervisor was autocratic, accepting suggestions from no one.*

automatic (au tuh má tik) [AUTO self + MAT to act]—operating by itself. *The car has automatic transmission.*

automation (aw tuh mā' shun) [AUTO self + MAT to act]—a system using self-operating machines. *The factory introduced automation and replaced many workers with robots.*

automaton (aw tom' uh tun) [AUTO self + MAT to act]—an apparatus that functions by itself; a robot. Also, a person who has lost all human qualities and acts mechanically. *Because she had been stapling pages for so many hours, she felt like an automaton.*

automobile (aw' tuh mō bēl) [AUTO self + MOB to move]—*lit.* a self-moving vehicle. *The Model T was one of the first automobiles.*

autonomic (aw tuh nom' ik) [AUTO self + NOM law]—pertaining to the autonomic nervous system, which acts according to its own (self) laws rather than through voluntary control. It regulates the heart, digestive system, and so forth. *He was trying to learn to control the actions of his autonomic nervous system through biofeedback.*

autonomous (aw ton' uh mus) [AUTO self + NOM law]—self-governing. *Released from state control, the college finally became autonomous.*

autonomy (aw ton' uh mē) [AUTO self + NOM law]—the right of self-government. *Many small nations are struggling for autonomy.*

autopsy (aw' top sē) [AUTO self + OP sight]—*lit.* a seeing for oneself; an examination of a dead body to discover the cause of death. *The autopsy revealed that the cause of death was a heart attack.*

ALSO: autobiography, autograph, automat

□EXERCISE 1   Write the appropriate AUTO word.

1. He was _____ in his control of the company, allowing his subordinates no power.
2. With her mind on more important matters, she performed her household tasks

   like an _____.
3. The people were tired of being ruled by an _____ and of having no say in their government.
4. They were threatening to revolt in the hope of changing their _____ to a democracy.
5. The digestion of food is controlled by the _____ nervous system.
6. A small group of workers broke away from the parent company and

   became _____.
7. When you walk into the room, an _____ switch turns on the electric light.

□EXERCISE 2   REVIEW   Write C in front of each sentence in which all words are used correctly.

_____ 1. A biennial meeting is one that is held every two years.

_____ 2. An anonymous note is a threatening note.

_____ 3. An annuity provides fixed payments at regular intervals.

_____ 4. An anthropoid animal resembles human beings.

_____ 5. The annals of a society are its yearly records.

_____ 6. He put up a good fight against his antagonist.

_____ 7. Ambivalence means having two conflicting emotions at the same time.

_____ 8. An agnostic does not believe in God.

_____ 9. The Vietnam War antedates World War II.

_____ 10. Antediluvian means old-fashioned.

_____ 11. The antiquarian looked through my books but found none new enough to interest him.

_____ 12. She arranged the photographs on the bulletin board in an asymmetrical pattern.

_____ 13. Biannual means occurring two times a year.

_____ 14. Antiquity means ancient times.

_____ 15. After days of traveling across Antarctica, the explorers finally reached the North Pole.

BENE—well, good

Words that begin with BENE always describe something *good*—an action, a result, or an attitude.

benediction (ben uh dik′ shun) [BENE good + DICT to speak]—*lit.* a speaking of good wishes; a blessing. *After the benediction the congregation filed out.*

benefactor (ben uh fak′ tur) [BENE good + FAC to do]—*lit.* one who does something good; one who gives help or financial assistance. *The college owed much to its generous benefactors.*

beneficence (buh nef′ uh suns) [BENE good + FAC to do]—*lit.* the doing of good; kindness; charity. *The scholarships were funded through the beneficence of the alumni.*

beneficial (ben uh fish′ ul) [BENE well + FAC to do]—producing benefits; advantageous. *Having a study schedule is beneficial.*

beneficiary (ben uh fish′ ē er ē) [BENE good + FAC to do]—a person who receives benefits, as from a will or an insurance policy. *He was the beneficiary of his father's will.*

benefit (ben′ uh fit) [BENE well + FAC to do]—anything that promotes well-being; a payment to one in need. *She got considerable benefit from her exercise program.*

benevolence (buh nev′ uh luns) [BENE well + VOL to wish]—an inclination to do good; a kindly or charitable act. *The benevolence of the church members was shown by their generous contributions to charity.*
    (Benevolence and beneficence are close synonyms.)

benevolent (buh nev′ uh lunt) [BENE well + VOL to wish]—*lit.* wishing someone well; inclined to do good. *The department manager had a benevolent attitude toward her staff, giving them days off now and then.*

benign (bi nīn′)—having a kindly (good) attitude or disposition. *The parents looked upon the capers of their son with benign tolerance.* Also, in medicine, mild in character; not malignant. *The growth proved to be benign rather than malignant.*
    (Benevolent and benign are close synonyms. Both mean having a kindly attitude, but benevolent often includes the idea of doing something charitable, and benign often has a medical meaning opposite to malignant.)

ALSO: beneficent

☐**EXERCISE 1**   Write the appropriate BENE word.

1. The congregation rose for the final _____.

2. A _____ of the university provided funds for medical research.

3. The scholarships were provided by the _____ of the alumni.

4. Fortunately they found that the tumor was _____.

5. This country has a _____ attitude toward developing nations, often giving them financial aid.

6. She was the _____ of her father's insurance policy.

7. The displaced families were provided for by the _____ of several charitable organizations.

8. He found a walk a day _____ to his health.

☐**EXERCISE 2   REVIEW**   Write C in front of each sentence in which all words are used correctly. Then in each remaining blank, write the word that should have been used.

_____ 1. The chimpanzees and other amphibians were playing in the trees.

_____ 2. When the children knocked at his door, the old misanthrope shouted for them to go away.

_____ 3. Instruments today can measure the functioning of the autonomic nervous system.

_____ 4. She received a stated salary per annum plus some bonuses.

_____ 5. The anthropology class was studying a Northwest Coast Indian culture.

_____ 6. Having no interest in his job, he worked like an automaton.

_____ 7. Prosperity is an antidote for political unrest.

_____ 8. After being a colony for years, the island finally achieved autonomy.

_____ 9. Six college scholarships were established through the philanthropy of a large commercial corporation.

☐**EXERCISE 3**   Are you adding a word or two each day to your WORD LIST on a blank page at the end of this book? Adding even one word a day will make a great difference in your word power.

BI—two

Back in the days of sailing ships, according to one story, the bread taken along on the voyages always became moldy. Then someone discovered that by baking the bread *twice,* enough moisture could be removed so that it remained edible during long voyages. The new kind of bread was called *biscuit* [BI two + COQUERE to cook] or *twice*-baked bread. Today biscuits are no longer twice-baked but are merely quick breads or non-yeast breads baked in small cakes.

bicameral (bī kam' ur ul) [BI two + CAMER chamber]—composed of two legislative chambers or branches. *The United States has a bicameral legislative system composed of the Senate and the House of Representatives.*

bicentennial (bī sen ten' ē ul) [BI two + CENT hundred + ENN year]—a 200th anniversary. *The United States celebrated its bicentennial in 1976.*

biceps (bī' seps) [BI two + CAPIT head]—any muscle having two heads or points of origin, as the large muscle at the front of the upper arm. *The wrestler flexed his biceps.*

bicuspid (bī kus' pid) [BI two + CUSPID point]—a tooth having two points. *A human adult has eight bicuspids.*

bicycle (bī' sik ul) [BI two + CYCL circle]—*lit.* two circles; a two-wheeled vehicle. *She rode her bicycle through the park.*

bigamy (big' uh mē) [BI two + GAM marriage]—marrying one person while legally married to another. *Bigamy is against the law in this country.*

bilateral (bī lat' ur ul) [BI two + LATER side]—having or involving two sides; binding on both parties (in contrast to unilateral in which only one party has an obligation). *According to a bilateral agreement, each of the two nations will cut armament expenditures.*

bilingual (bī ling' gwul) [BI two + LINGU language]—able to use two languages. *In Canada job opportunities are greater for a bilingual person.*

binoculars (bu nahk' yuh lurs) [BI two + OCUL eye]—field glasses for use with two eyes (in contrast to the telescope, which is for use with one eye only). *He watched the blue jay through his binoculars.*

bipartisan (bī pahr' tuh zun)—consisting of or supported by two parties, especially two major political parties. *Assured of bipartisan support, the senator was confident the bill would pass.*

biped (bī' ped) [BI two + PED foot]—a two-footed animal. *Humans are the only bipeds who laugh.*

biscuit (bis' kut) [BI two + COQUERE to cook]—*lit.* twice-cooked or baked; today a quick bread baked in small pieces. *Please pass the biscuits.*

bisect (bī' sekt) [BI two + SECT to cut]—to cut in two, as a diameter bisects a circle. *The nature trail bisects the park.*

bivalve (bī' valv)—a mollusk having two valves or shells hinged together, as a mussell or clam. *The oyster is a bivalve that is valued by both gourmets and jewelers.*

ALSO: biannual, biennial, bifocal, bigamist, binomial, bipartite

☐**EXERCISE 1** Write the appropriate BI word.

1. The two nations signed a _____ trade agreement.

2. The committee was _____, composed of representatives from both political parties.

3. Laws must be passed by both houses in our _____ system.

4. The pinkish angel wing shells are the attractive outer covering of a

   _____.

5. The new highway will _____ the city, bringing more business to downtown stores.

6. The athlete was proud of his strong _____.

7. With her _____ she was able to get an excellent view of the races.

8. A _____ celebration occurs every two hundred years.

9. She is _____, speaking both English and French fluently.

10. When it was discovered that he had two wives at the same time, a charge

    of _____ was brought against him.

11. A tooth ending in two points is called a _____.

12. Men and monkeys are both _____.

☐**EXERCISE 2** In your vocabulary journal write several sentences that you might use if you were writing a paper about the Civil War. Use some of these words: annals, antebellum, antedates, benign, benefactor.

BIO—life

The root BIO meaning *life* combines with SYM meaning *together* to form an interesting word—**symbiosis,** the living together of two dissimilar organisms, usually for the benefit of both. For example, the hermit crab lives among the lethal tentacles of the sea anemone and is protected from its enemies by the stinging power of the tentacles. The anemone, on the other hand, is carried in the claws or on the back of the hermit crab to new feeding grounds. Thus the symbiosis is beneficial to both.

autobiography (awt uh bī ahg′ ru fē) [AUTO self + BIO life + GRAPH to write]—an account of a person's life written by that person. *The Autobiography of Benjamin Franklin is a classic.*

biodegradable (bī ō di grā′ duh bul)—capable of being broken down by living microorganisms and absorbed by the environment. *She switched to a biodegradable detergent, which would not pollute the streams.*

biofeedback (bī ō fēd′ bak)—a technique for consciously regulating a bodily (life) function thought to be involuntary, as heartbeat or blood pressure, by using an instrument to monitor the function and to signal changes in it. *She found that she could slow her pulse by using biofeedback.*

biography (bī ahg′ ru fē) [BIO life + GRAPH to write]—a written account of someone's life. *Carl Sandburg wrote in his biography of Lincoln: "When he kept store he often held an open book in his hand, reading five or ten minutes, closing the book to wait on a customer or to tell a story, then opening the book and reading in spite of the babblings of the men drying their mittens by the fire."*

biology (bī ahl′ uh jē) [BIO life + LOGY study of]—the study of plant and animal life. *Biology includes botany and zoology.*

biopsy (bī′ op sē) [BIO life + OP sight]—*lit.* a seeing of live tissues; the examination of tissues removed from the living body. *The biopsy revealed that the growth was benign.*

biosphere (bī′ uh sfir)—the part of the earth, extending from its crust out into the surrounding atmosphere, in which living things exist. *Many parts of the biosphere remain to be explored.*

symbiosis (sim bi ō′ sis) [SYM together + BIO life]—the living together in close union of two dissimilar organisms, often to their mutual benefit. *The symbiosis of algae and fungi forms lichens.*

symbiotic (sim bi ot′ ik) [SYM together + BIO life]—living together in a close relationship, often to the benefit of both. *In a symbiotic relationship, ants protect defenseless aphids and then "milk" them for their honeydew.*

ALSO: amphibian, antibiotic, biochemistry, bionic, microbe

☐**EXERCISE 1** These sentences include not only words with the BIO root but also words with roots you have previously studied. First write C in front of each sentence in which all words are used correctly. Then in each remaining blank, write the word that should have been used.

_____ 1. Parts of the earth's biosphere are inhabited only by microorganisms.

_____ 2. The symbiotic relationship of ants and aphids is beneficial to both.

_____ 3. Thus the relationship of the ants and aphids is an example of symbiosis.

_____ 4. Through the beneficence of the alumni, the college was able to offer ten scholarships.

_____ 5. The bilateral professor could speak two languages.

_____ 6. A bivalve is a two-footed animal.

_____ 7. To determine the type of tumor, the doctor performed a biopsy.

_____ 8. My teenage brother is an anomaly; he doesn't like video games.

_____ 9. The dentist found a cavity in one bicuspid.

_____ 10. The wrestler flexed his biceps in preparation for the match.

_____ 11. I've been reading about the antebellum Underground Railroad, which helped slaves escape to the North.

_____ 12. According to the annals of the college, the administration building was erected in 1920.

_____ 13. The attempt to control involuntary bodily functions is called ambiguity.

_____ 14. My grandmother loves to tell little anecdotes from her childhood.

_____ 15. The youngster was amoral because he had grown up without any character training.

_____ 16. The lawyer's ambiguous statements made me think he wasn't being straightforward.

_____ 17. My car is definitely antediluvian.

_____ 18. In an autocracy one person rules.

CHRON—time

Like all CHRON words, **anachronism** has something to do with *time*. It's the term applied to anything that is out of its proper historical *time*. For example, it would be an anachronism to mention antibiotics in writing about the nineteenth century.

Shakespeare let several anachronisms slip into his plays. He speaks of a clock striking in *Julius Caesar,* but striking clocks had not been invented at the time of Julius Caesar. And in *King John* he mentions using cannons, but the scenes in that play took place many years before cannons were used in England.

anachronism (un nak' ruh niz um) [ANA back + CHRON time]—anything out of its proper historical time. *To include an electric typewriter in a story set in 1920 would be an anachronism.*

chronic (kron' ik)—continuing for a long time, as a chronic disease. *A chronic complainer, he was never happy with his situation.*

chronicle (kron' i kul)—an account of events arranged in order of time. The Anglo-Saxon Chronicle *gives an account of twelve centuries of British history.*

chronological (kron uh loj' i kul)—arranged in order of time of occurrence. *The play dramatizes in chronological order the events that led to the bombing of Pearl Harbor.*

chronology (kruh nol' uh jē) [CHRON time + -LOGY study of]—a list of events arranged according to time of occurrence. *He had memorized the chronology of the reigns of the English monarchs.*

chronometer (kruh nom' uh tur) [CHRON time + METER measure]—an instrument for measuring time precisely, especially in navigation. *Before making an entry in the log, the captain consulted the chronometer.*

synchronize (sin' kruh nīz) [SYN together + CHRON time]—to cause to operate (keep time) in unison, as to synchronize watches or to synchronize the sound with the film in a motion picture. *The sound track of the film was not synchronized with the picture.*

☐**EXERCISE 1**   Write the appropriate CHRON word.

1. We made a _____ list of the trips we had taken during the last three years.
2. Pedal cars are an _____ in *The Flintstones,* a cartoon series set in the Stone Age.

3. Let's _____ our watches so that we can meet for lunch.

4. The _____ is only one of many precision instruments on a ship.
5. I borrow money from my friends so often that they say my empty pockets are

   a _____ condition.

☐**EXERCISE 2   REVIEW**   Underline the appropriate word.

1. Her family had to listen patiently every evening to a (chronicle, chronometer) of all her achievements that day.

2. The absence of government is called (autocracy, anarchy).

3. In a (bilateral, bicameral) system of government, one legislative body acts as a check on the other.

4. They decided to spend their savings on some beautiful (antiquated, antique) furniture.

5. The museum in Atlanta is an old mansion of (antiquarian, antebellum) days.

6. It would be an (ambiguity, anachronism) to describe walking on the moon in a story set in 1950.

7. His (beneficent, misanthropic) attitude toward his fellow workers made him disliked by everyone.

8. The patient was trying to learn to control her autonomic nervous system through (biopsy, biofeedback).

9. After a long struggle to free itself from foreign rule, the small country finally became (autonomous, autocratic)

CIRCUM—around

CIRCUM always means *around*. A **circumference** is the outer boundary line *around* a circular area. To **circumnavigate** the globe is to go *around* it. A **circumstance** [CIRCUM around + STA to stand] is literally something standing *around*. Perhaps the circumstance that is standing *around* and keeping you from going to a movie is a lack of money.

circuit (sur' kit)—the regular journey around a territory by a person performing duties. *The newspaper boy made his usual circuit.* Also, a closed path followed by an electric current. *When the circuit was interrupted, the lights went out.* Also, an arrangement of electrically or electromagnetically connected components. *Computers use integrated circuits.*

circuitous (sur kyoo' uh tus)—roundabout; winding. *Because she didn't know the way, she took us by a rather circuitous route. His speech was full of circuitous arguments that led nowhere.*

circumference (sur kum' furnts) [CIRCUM around + FER to carry]—*lit.* a line carried around; the outer boundary line around a circular area. *In our math class we learned how to find the circumference of a circle.*

circumlocution (sur kum lō kyoo' shun) [CIRCUM around + LOC to speak]—a roundabout way of saying something. *Saying "A number of other commitments will make it impossible for me to find the time to attend the meeting" would be a circumlocution for the simple statement "I can't attend the meeting."*

circumnavigate (sur kum nav' uh gāt) [CIRCUM around + NAV to sail]—to sail around. *Magellan was the first person to circumnavigate the globe.*

circumscribe (sur' kum skrīb) [CIRCUM around + SCRIB to write]—*lit.* to write a line around the bounds; to limit; to confine. *The rules of the private school circumscribed the daily activities of the students.*

circumspect (sur' kum spekt) [CIRCUM around + SPEC to look]—cautious; careful to consider possible consequences. *She was circumspect in making suggestions to her temperamental boss.*

circumstance (sur' kum stants) [CIRCUM around + STA to stand]—*lit.* something standing around; a fact or event accompanying another fact or event. *Because of the circumstances at home, I had to give up the trip I had planned.*

circumvent (sur kum vent') [CIRCUM around + VEN to come]—*lit.* to come around; to get around or to overcome by artful maneuvering; to prevent. *By offering a small wage increase, the management hoped to circumvent a walkout.*

☐**EXERCISE 1** Write the appropriate CIRCUM word.

1. "He does not exhibit the self-control appropriate to his age" is simply a

   _____ for "He's a brat."
2. He opposed the plan and did all he could to _____ it.

3. Because she didn't want to offend anyone, she was always _____
   about offering advice.
4. Don't let all the rules _____ your creativity.

5. We followed a _____ path up the mountain.

6. Philippe Jeantot set a world record when he _____ the
   globe solo in his sailboat in 159 days in 1983.

☐**EXERCISE 2 REVIEW** Write C in front of each sentence in which all words
are used correctly.

_____ 1. I didn't really want to hear a chronological account of his day's activities.

_____ 2. Pollution is causing changes in parts of the biosphere.

_____ 3. The Nuclear Waste Policy Act of 1982 passed with bipartisan support.

_____ 4. Plastic containers, which are not biodegradable, are cluttering the coun-
         tryside.

_____ 5. We synchronized our watches and agreed to meet at eight.

_____ 6. Various philanthropic organizations came to the aid of the flood victims.

_____ 7. A bicentennial celebration was held at the end of the club's first one
         hundred years.

_____ 8. To bisect an apple is to cut it in four pieces.

_____ 9. His standing up and speaking at the meeting was atypical.

☐**EXERCISE 3** Turn the following circumlocution into a concise statement.

   With reference to your letter, I wish to inform you that we have taken your
complaint under consideration and have come to the conclusion that the TV set
that you purchased from our company should be repaired by us free of charge.

_____

_____

COM, CON, COL, COR—together, with

Companion takes on new meaning when we learn its roots. A companion [COM with + PAN bread] was originally a person one shared one's bread *with*. We don't think of that original meaning today, and yet when we want to be hospitable, we invite our companions to share our food.

COM meaning *together* or *with* is sometimes difficult to spot because it so often changes its last letter to be like the first letter of the root following it. Thus COMloquial becomes COLloquial, COMnect becomes CONnect, and COMrelate becomes CORrelate. Sometimes the letter *m* is dropped completely, and COMeducation becomes COeducation. Changing the last letter in these ways makes the pronunciation easier. On page 6 is a further discussion of changes in root spelling.

Sometimes, as in **condone** and **compunction**, COM is used merely as an intensive, giving more emphasis to the root that follows.

coherent (kō hir' unt) [CO together + HER to stick]—*lit.* sticking together; having an orderly relation of parts. *My geology professor's lectures are always coherent and interesting.*

collaborate (kuh lab' uh rāt)—to labor together. *Two committee members are collaborating in preparing the report.*

collusion (kuh lōō' zhun) [COL together + LUD to play]—*lit.* playing together; a secret agreement between two or more persons for a deceitful purpose. *The manager suspected collusion between the two employees accused of embezzling company funds.*

commensurate (kuh men' suh rit) [COM together + MENS to measure]—*lit.* measured together; equal in measure or size; proportionate. *The pay should be commensurate with the work.*

commiserate (kuh miz' uh rāt) [COM with + MISERARI to pity]—to sympathize. *She commiserated with me over the loss of my job.*

committee (kuh mit' ē) [COM together + MIT to send]—a group of people sent to meet together to consider some matter. *A committee was appointed to plan the program.*

commodious (kuh mō' dē us) [COM with + MOD measure]—with plenty of room; spacious. *Their mobile home was more commodious than I had anticipated.*

commotion (kuh mō' shun) [COM together + MOT to move]—people moving together; social disorder. *What's all the commotion?*

companion (kum pan' yun) [COM with + PAN bread]—*lit.* a person one shares one's bread with; a comrade. *His dog was his faithful companion.*

complicate (kahm' pluh kāt) [COM together + PLIC to fold]—*lit.* to fold together; to make intricate or involved. *Talking about finances will merely complicate the discussion.*

composition (kahm puh zish′ un) [COM together + POS to put]—a putting together of parts to form a whole. *I was finally satisfied with the composition I had written.*

compress (kum pres′) [COM together + PRES to press]—to press or squeeze together. *I'm going to compress my essay into two pages.*

compunction (kum pungk′ shun) [COM (intensive) + PUNCT to prick]—*lit.* a prick of conscience; an uneasiness caused by a sense of guilt; a slight regret. *He felt some compunction about taking so much of his tutor's time.*

computer (kum pyoo′ tur) [COM together + PUTARE to reckon]—an electronic machine that performs high-speed mathematical and logical calculations when given coded information. *I use my computer to do my math problems.*

condominium (kahn duh min′ ē uhm) [CON together + DOMINIUM ownership]—a building in which the living units are owned individually and the grounds are owned together. *Because they didn't want to take care of a yard, they bought a condominium instead of a house.*

condone (kun dōn′) [COM (intensive) + DON to give]—to forgive or overlook (an offense). *The public can't condone the dishonest dealings of the company representative.*

congenital (kun jen′ uh tul) [CON together + GEN birth]—*lit.* born together; existing at birth. *The child has a congenital heart defect.*

consensus (kun sen′ sus) [CON together + SENS to feel]—*lit.* a feeling together; general agreement. *No consensus has been reached about the safety of nuclear plants.*

consummate (kun sum′ it) [CON together + SUMMA sum]—*lit.* summed up together; complete or perfect in every respect. *She was a consummate artist.* Also, complete; utter, as a consummate bore.

contemporary (kun tem′ puh rer ē) [CON together + TEMPOR time]—*lit.* together in time; belonging to the same age. *We're studying some contemporary novelists as well as those from the past.*

convene (kun vēn′) [CON together + VEN to come]—to come together formally. *The committee will convene next week.*

convention (kun ven′ chun) [CON together + VEN to come]—the coming together of the members of a group. *The State Teachers Convention is being held next week.*

convivial (kun viv′ ē ul) [CON together + VIV to live]—fond of eating, drinking, and being sociable together. *In a convivial mood, the guests stayed until midnight.*

correlate (kor′ uh lāt)—to relate together; to show relationship. *The accountant is trying to correlate this year's figures with last year's.*

ALSO: colloquial, colloquium, complacent, compulsive, concoction, concord, concourse, concur, concurrent, conducive, congregation, conjugal, conscription, conversant, corrupt

□**EXERCISE 1**   Write the appropriate COM word.

1. His rate of promotion has not been _____ with his hard work.

2. The management won't _____ such sloppy work.

3. Her grades did not _____ with her IQ score.

4. He's a _____ salesperson, the best in the company.

5. I felt no _____ about missing that meeting.

6. When their twins were born, they moved to a more _____ apartment.

7. No one was there to _____ with her when she needed sympathy most.

8. They traced the loss to _____ between two dishonest aides.

9. The _____ of the committee was that more funds should be given to the private school.

10. The two engineers will _____ on the project.

11. The child's inability to speak was traced to a _____ defect.

12. They paid more for their _____ than they would have for a house.

13. Completely upset, she couldn't give a _____ account of the accident.

14. The committee will stop for lunch and _____ again at two.

15. Everyone at the party was in a _____ mood.

□**EXERCISE 2**   In your journal write a few sentences describing an imaginary party and using these words: condominium, commodious, contemporary, ambience, convivial.

□**EXERCISE 3 REVIEW** In this paragraph are nine words you've studied.

1. First read the paragraph and underline those nine words.

   Last weekend our biology class went to the lake to study bivalves, amphibians, and various other forms of marine life. On our way there we took a circuitous route through a wooded area and were dismayed to find the roadside cluttered with bottles, plastic cartons, and other trash that isn't biodegradable. People seem ambivalent about our natural scenery. They like a beautiful countryside, yet they clutter it. They wouldn't condone messiness in their own yards, yet they feel no compunction about tossing a bottle or a candy wrapper into the woods. It's a perennial problem, and it will be solved only when each individual develops a responsible attitude toward our natural scenery.

2. Now write on the lines below any of the nine words whose meaning you are not quite sure of.

3. Next look up each of the doubtful words in the Word Index on page 149. There you will find the number of the page where the word is explained.

4. When you are sure of the meaning of all the doubtful words, reread the paragraph and see how much more satisfying it is to read a paragraph in which you are sure of every word.

_____

_____

_____

_____

_____

CRED—to believe

In the Middle Ages it was customary for the servants to carry the prepared food from the kitchen to a small side table in the dining hall,
where, in front of the master and his guests, one of the servants would
taste the food to show that it was not spoiled or poisoned. This side table
came to be called a credence (belief or trust), and still today in France
a side table is called a *crédence* and in Italy a *credenza*. And today in
the U.S. a side table is sometimes called a *credenza*. Our English word
credence no longer refers to our trust in the food we eat, but we still
speak of having credence (belief or trust) in what we read and in what
people tell us.

Note how the following CRED words go in pairs:

credible—believable
incredible—unbelievable

credulous—believing too readily
incredulous—not believing readily

credulity—tendency to believe readily
incredulity—tendency not to believe readily

credence (krē′ duns)—belief; acceptance as true. *They should not have given
   any credence to the rumor.*
credentials (kri den′ shuls)—documents that cause others to believe in one.
   The credentials she brought from her last job were excellent.
credibility (kred uh bil′ uh tē)—trustworthiness. *No one ever questioned his
   credibility.*
credible (kred′ uh bul)—believable. *He gave a credible explanation for his
   tardiness.*
credit (kred′ ut)—trust, as financial credit; a source of honor, as a credit to
   one's family. *She always paid cash rather than asking for credit.*
credulity (kri doo′ li tē)—tendency to believe readily on too little evidence;
   gullibility. *Her credulity made her an easy prey for anyone with a
   hard luck story.*
credulous (krej′ uh lus)—believing too readily on too little evidence; gull-
   ible. *Only a credulous person would be taken in by such ads.*
creed (krēd)—a formal statement of religious or other belief, as the creed of
   a church. *She learned to repeat the Apostles' Creed.*
discredit (dis kred′ ut) [DIS not + CRED to believe]—*lit.* not to believe;
   to distrust; to destroy belief in. *Because the newspaper articles had
   discredited the mayor, he resigned.*
incredible (in kred′ uh bul) [IN not + CRED to believe]—unbelievable.
   The amount of work she could do in an hour was incredible.

incredulity (in kri d$\overline{oo}$' li tē) [IN not + CRED to believe]—tendency not to believe readily; skepticism. *As he listened to their excuses, his incredulity was obvious.*

incredulous (in krej' uh lus) [IN not + CRED to believe]—not believing readily; disbelieving. *When she heard she had won the prize, she was incredulous.*

miscreant (mis' krē unt) [MIS less + CRED to believe]—originally, an unbeliever in religion; now, an evildoer or criminal. *The police were trying to round up the miscreants.*

ALSO: accreditation, accredited, creditor

◻EXERCISE 1 Match each word with its definition.

A. creed   C. credulous   E. credence
B. incredible   D. incredulous   F. miscreant

_____ 1. unbelievable

_____ 2. believing too readily

_____ 3. not believing readily

_____ 4. acceptance as true

_____ 5. a declaration of one's beliefs

_____ 6. an evildoer or criminal

◻EXERCISE 2 Write the appropriate CRED word.

1. The excuse he gave was simply not _____.
2. As some of the jurors began frowning, the lawyer became aware of their

   _____.

3. I wouldn't give any _____ to such a poorly documented report.
4. The _____ has so far evaded the police.
5. When they heard that their son had left the city, they were _____.

6. All his big stories taxed my _____.

7. I'm not so _____ as to believe all I'm told.

8. On his trek through the Arctic, he endured _____ hardships.
9. The jury questioned the _____ of the witness.

10. He had to produce _____ before he was allowed to enter the courtroom.

CUR—to run

If you find it difficult to hang on to your money, don't be surprised because the word **currency** means literally *running*. The currency in circulation in a country is constantly *running* from person to person. And if currency should *run* through the hands of a person or a company too rapidly, it might be the **precursor** [PRE before + CUR to run] or forerunner of bankruptcy.

concourse (kon′ kōrs) [CON together + CUR to run]—*lit.* a running together; a large open space where crowds gather. *The main concourse in the airport was filled with tourists.*

concur (kon kur′) [CON together + CUR to run]—*lit.* to run together; to agree. *We all concurred with the recommendation of the committee.*

concurrent (kun kur′ unt) [CON together + CUR to run]—*lit.* running together; occurring at the same time. *The town council and the school board held concurrent meetings.*

courier (kur′ ē ur) [CUR to run]—one who carries (runs with) messages. *The courier arrived with the letter.*

course (kōrs′) [CUR to run]—a running onward from one point to the next, as the course of a stream; in education, a series of studies leading (running) toward a degree. *I like all the courses required for my major.*

currency (kur′ un sē) [CUR to run]—money that passes (runs) from person to person in a country. *The currency in that country is mostly silver.*

current (kur′ unt) [CUR to run]—the flow (running) of water or air or electricity; prevalent at the moment (running along), as current fashions. *The current trend is toward smaller cars.*

curriculum (kuh rik′ yuh lum) [CUR to run]—originally, a race course; today, all the courses offered by an educational institution. *The curriculum offers me a wide choice of courses.*

cursive (kur′ siv) [CUR to run]—*lit.* running along; handwriting with the letters joined together. *She preferred to use printing rather than cursive writing.*

cursory (kur′ suh rē)—running over rapidly without attention to detail; hasty and superficial. *She gave the novel only a cursory reading.*

discourse (dis′ kōrs) [DIS apart + CUR to run]—*lit.* to run about; to speak at length; a formal and lengthy discussion of a subject. *He gave a discourse on Ibsen's symbolism.*

excursion (ik skur′ zhun) [EX out + CUR to run]—*lit.* a running out somewhere; a short journey. *We took a day's excursion down the river.*

occur (uh kur′) [OB toward + CUR to run]—*lit.* to run toward; to take place; to happen. *I was amazed at what had occurred.*

precursor (pri kur′ sur) [PRE before + CUR to run]—a person or thing that runs before; a forerunner. *The fountain pen was the precursor of the ballpoint.*

recourse (rē′ kōrs) [RE back + CUR to run]—*lit.* a running back (for help):

a turning to someone or something for help. *His only recourse was to notify the police.*

recur (ri kur′) [RE again + CUR to run]—*lit.* to run again; to happen again. *If the problem should recur, you'll have to buy a new battery.*

recurrent (ri kur′ unt) [RE back + CUR to run]—*lit.* running back: returning repeatedly. *They still had the recurrent problem of absenteeism.*

ALSO: concurrence, corridor, incur, incursion, occurrence

☐**EXERCISE 1** Match each word with its definition.

A. recur   C. concurrent   E. precursor
B. recourse   D. cursory   F. concourse

_____ 1. a turning to someone or something for aid

_____ 2. a large open space where crowds gather

_____ 3. hasty and superficial

_____ 4. to happen again

_____ 5. occurring at the same time

_____ 6. a forerunner

☐**EXERCISE 2** Write the appropriate CUR word.

1. A _____ glance at the program told her the music would not be rock.
2. Because the two meetings were _____, she couldn't attend both.
3. His _____ attacks of asthma led him to go to a specialist.
4. I _____ with all your suggestions and will help you carry them out.
5. I was surprised that he always used printing rather than _____ writing in his letters.
6. Since no one could tell me anything about the author, my only

   _____ was to contact the publisher.
7. On the prairies, the blossoming crocuses are a welcome _____ of spring.
8. Hundreds of waiting passengers filled the airport _____.
9. He bored us with another of his _____ on the value of free trade.
10. He hoped that listening to ghost stories around the campfire wouldn't cause

    his former nightmares to _____.

DEM—people

Many words have changed their meanings over the centuries, some having changed so much that they now mean almost the opposite of what they meant originally. **Demagogue** is an example. First used at the time of the Peloponnesian War, the word demagogue (DEM people + AGOG leader) referred to a leader or orator who championed the cause of the common *people* of Athens in their fight against the aristocrats of Sparta. Gradually through the years, however, such leaders began pursuing their own interests rather than helping the people, and today a demagogue is a political leader who makes impassioned appeals to the emotions and prejudices of *people* to gain personal power.

demagogue (dem' uh gog) [DEM people + AGOG leader]—originally, a leader of the common people; now, a leader who stirs up the people by appealing to their emotions and prejudices to win them over quickly and thus gain power. *Interested only in gaining personal power, the senator was a demagogue.*

demagoguery (dem' uh gog uh rē) [DEM people + AGOG leader]—the methods or practices of a demagogue. *Her campaign speech was pure demagoguery.*

democracy (di mahk' ru sē) [DEM people + CRAC to rule]—*lit.* people rule; government by representatives elected by the people. *More countries are now voting for democracy.*

demographic (dem uh graf' ik) [DEM people + GRAPH to write]—*lit.* writing about people; pertaining to the study of human populations, especially their density, distribution, and vital statistics. *The 1990 census gathered a wealth of demographic information.*

endemic (en dem' ik) [EN in + DEM people]—native to a particular people or country, as an endemic disease, which occurs only among certain people, or an endemic plant or animal, which is found only in a certain location. *The snail darter, an endangered species, is endemic to the Little Tennessee River.*

epidemic (ep uh dem' ik) [EPI upon + DEM people]—*lit.* upon the people; a disease or other abnormal condition spreading rapidly among many people. *The flu epidemic caused many absences from work.*

pandemic (pan dem' ik) [PAN all + DEM people]—*lit.* among all the people; widespread. *The economic depression was pandemic.*

ALSO: democrat, democratic, demography

□**EXERCISE 1**   Write the appropriate DEM word.

1. The eucalyptus tree is _____ to Australia, but years ago it was brought to California, where it now grows in many areas.

2. The politician was really a _____, seeking to advance his own interests.

3. People no longer have to fear a polio _____.

4. Malaria is _____ in the tropics.

5. _____ information is helpful in choosing the best location for a new business.

6. Because he had no concrete proposals to offer, the politician resorted to

   _____ to try to win votes.

□**EXERCISE 2   REVIEW**   Give the meaning of each root and a word in which it is found.

	MEANING	WORD
1. A, AN	_____	_____
2. AMBI, AMPHI	_____	_____
3. ANN, ENN	_____	_____
4. ANTE, ANTI	_____	_____
5. ANTHROP	_____	_____
6. ANTI	_____	_____
7. AUTO	_____	_____
8. BENE	_____	_____
9. BI	_____	_____
10. BIO	_____	_____
11. CHRON	_____	_____
12. CIRCUM	_____	_____
13. COM, CON, COL, COR	_____	_____

DICT—to speak

The word addict has had a long history. In Roman law, to addict a person meant to turn that person over to a master by sentence *(speaking)* of the court. Through the years addict has kept something of its old meaning in that it now refers to turning oneself over to a habit, which can, of course, be a master.

abdicate (ab′ di kāt) [AB away + DICT to speak, proclaim]—*lit.* to proclaim away; to renounce formally a throne or high office. *The king abdicated.*

addict (uh dikt′) [AD to + DICT to speak]—*lit.* to speak to or to sentence oneself; to give oneself habitually or compulsively to something. *He was addicted to alcohol.*

contradict (kahn tru dikt′) [CONTRA against + DICT to speak]—to speak against; to assert the opposite of what someone has said. *I didn't dare contradict her.*

dictate (dik′ tāt)—to speak or read something aloud to be recorded by another; to give (speak) orders or commands. *The boss dictates his letters slowly.*

dictator (dik′ tāt ur)—one whose speech is to be taken as the final word; one who orders others around; a tyrannical ruler. *The small country was ruled by a dictator.*

dictatorial (dik tu tōr′ ē ul)—speaking and acting in a domineering or oppressive way. *The crew resented the dictatorial manner of the foreman.*

diction (dik′ shun)—choice of words in speaking or writing. *She used excellent diction, always choosing exactly the right word.* Also, enunciation in speaking or singing. *His diction was so clear that he could be understood at the back of the auditorium.*

dictionary (dik′ shu ner ē)—a book containing the words of a (spoken) language. *I'd be lost without my dictionary.*

dictum (dik′ tum)—a formal and authoritative statement (speech). *After hearing the dictum of the chairperson, the committee members knew what they had to do.*

edict (ē′ dikt) [E out + DICT to speak]—*lit.* a speaking out; an official decree. *The Edict of Nantes granted toleration to Protestants in France.*

jurisdiction (joor us dik′ shun) [JURIS law + DICT to speak]—the right to interpret (speak) and apply the law; legal power to hear and decide cases; the extent of such judicial or other authority. *The case was not within the court's jurisdiction.*

predict (pri dikt′) [PRE before + DICT to speak]—*lit.* to speak beforehand; to foretell. *The Bureau of Meteorology is predicting a late spring.*

valedictorian (val uh dik tōr′ ē un) [VALE farewell + DICT to speak]— a student, usually of the highest scholastic standing, who gives the farewell speech at commencement. *As valedictorian of her class, she gave a good speech at graduation.*

ALSO: addiction, benediction, ditto, interdict, malediction, verdict

---

☐**EXERCISE 1** Write the appropriate DICT word.

1. The judge was overwhelmed by the number of cases in her ＿＿＿＿＿＿.

2. She was trying to improve her ＿＿＿＿＿＿＿＿＿ by taking a course in public speaking.

3. The head of the committee was ＿＿＿＿＿＿＿＿＿, always trying to force decisions.

4. When the king ＿＿＿＿＿＿＿＿＿, his son took the throne.

5. The residents of the island were granted citizenship by an ＿＿＿＿＿＿＿ of the colonial government.

6. After the president's ＿＿＿＿＿＿＿＿＿ about absenteeism, the employees complied with the new stricter rules.

7. His long hours of study paid off, and he became the ＿＿＿＿＿＿＿＿＿ of his class.

8. She was ＿＿＿＿＿＿＿＿＿ to soap operas, spending most of her time watching them.

☐**EXERCISE 2 REVIEW** What word names or describes each of the following?

1. a study of the cultural development of human beings ＿＿＿＿＿＿＿＿＿

2. anything out of its proper historical time ＿＿＿＿＿＿＿＿＿

3. someone who benefits from a gift or a will ＿＿＿＿＿＿＿＿＿

4. a two-footed animal ＿＿＿＿＿＿＿＿＿

5. unable to distinguish between right and wrong ＿＿＿＿＿＿＿＿＿

6. marriage to a person while legally married to another ＿＿＿＿＿＿＿＿＿

☐**EXERCISE 3** In your journal write a few sentences describing a sports event and using some of these words: biannual, amphitheater, binoculars, anticlimax, consensus.

DIS, DI, DIF—not, away, apart

It was important in Roman times to start a journey or begin a new venture on a lucky day. One way to find out whether a day was favorable was to consult the stars. If the stars were *not* in a favorable position, the outcome of any undertaking begun on that day was certain to be a **disaster** (DIS not + ASTER star).

disarray (dis uh rā′) [DIS not + AREER to array]—*lit.* not arrayed or arranged properly; a state of disorder or confusion; disorderly dress. *Following the death of their leader, the political group fell into disarray.*

disaster (dis as′ tur) [DIS not + ASTER star]—*lit.* the stars not in a favorable position; a misfortune. *My score on that exam was a disaster.*

disburse (dis burs′) [DIS away + BURSA a purse]—*lit.* to take away from a purse; to pay out, as from a fund. *The president of the society disbursed the scholarship funds.*

discomfit (dis kum′ fit) [DIS not + COM together + FAC to do]—*lit.* to undo; to thwart the plans of; to make uneasy. *The leader felt discomfited because his motives were being questioned.*

disconcert (dis kun surt′) [DIS not + CONCERT to bring into agreement]—to upset; to frustrate. *The speaker was disconcerted by the noise in the balcony.*

(Disconcert and discomfit are close synonyms.)

disconsolate (dis kon′ suh lit)—not able to be consoled; hopelessly sad. *The team member responsible for losing the relay was disconsolate.*

discordant (dis kor′ dunt) [DIS apart + CORD heart]—*lit.* hearts apart; not in accord; disagreeable to the ear. *One discordant voice can ruin a choir.*

disease (diz ēz′) [DIS not + AISE ease]—*lit.* not at ease; illness. *Her disease is not communicable.*

dismantle (dis mant′ ul) [DIS apart + MANTEL cloak]—originally, to take a man's cloak off his back; to strip a house of furnishings; to take apart. *I dismantled the room for the painters.*

disparate (dis par′ ut) [DIS not + PAR equal]—*lit.* not equal; unlike. *The reporter wrote on subjects as disparate as ice hockey and women's fashions.*

disparity (di spar′ uh tē) [DIS not + PAR equal]—difference; unlikeness. *In spite of the disparity in their ages, they get along well.*

display (dis plā′) [DIS apart + PLIC to fold]—*lit.* to fold apart or unfold; to show. *The winning posters were on display.*

disproportionate (dis pruh pōr′ shun it)—not proportionate; out of proportion in size, shape, or amount. *His salary was disproportionate to the amount of work he did.*

dissect (dis ekt′) [DIS apart + SECT to cut]—to cut apart, especially for anatomical study. *Our class dissected frogs yesterday.*

disseminate (di sem′ uh nāt) [DIS apart + SEMIN seed]—to spread abroad as if sowing seed. *The publication disseminated information about endangered species.*

dissent (di sent') [DIS apart + SENT to feel]—to differ in opinion or feeling; to withhold approval. *If too many members dissent, the motion will not pass.*

dissident (dis' uh dunt) [DIS apart + SID to sit]—*lit.* sitting apart; one who disagrees; a dissenter. *The dissidents made trouble for the ruling party.*

dissuade (di swād') [DIS away + SUAD to persuade]—to turn a person away (from a course) by persuasion. *Finally they dissuaded him from giving up his job.*

distract (dis tråkt) [DIS apart + TRACT to draw]—to draw away the attention. *He tried to distract her attention from the accident.*

diverse (di vurs') [DI away + VERS to turn]—*lit.* turned away from each other; unlike, as diverse opinions. *The committee listened to all the diverse views.*

diversion (duh vur' zyun) [DI away + VERS to turn]—something that turns the mind away and relaxes or entertains. *Her favorite diversion is golf.*

divorce (duh vors') [DI away + VERS to turn]—*lit.* a turning away (in different directions); a dissolution of a marriage. *After the divorce, they were still friends.*

ALSO: diffident, diffuse, discord, discourse, discredit, discrepancy, discursive, dismiss, disparage, dispel, dispense, disrupt, dissolution, dissonant, distort, diversity, divert

---

☐**EXERCISE 1** Write the appropriate DIS word.

1. No one could _____ him from his goal.
2. Because she had not expected visitors, her house was in _____.

3. The club members couldn't agree on how to _____ the funds they had raised.
4. The cult was trying to _____ its views through door-to-door canvassing.
5. The movie director was _____ (or _____) by the bad reviews.

6. He _____ the room in preparation for a thorough cleaning.
7. There was considerable _____ between the brochure's description of the condominium and its reality.
8. The two students were writing on widely _____ subjects.

9. One _____ note marred an otherwise beautiful solo.

EQU—equal

If you're looking for a climate that's *equally* pleasant in summer and winter, you're looking for an **equable** climate. If you're eager for spring, you're waiting for the spring **equinox,** when days and nights are *equal.* If you want a fair settlement of a legal case, you want an **equitable** settlement. And if you can remain *equally* calm and composed under pleasant or unpleasant circumstances, you're able to maintain your **equanimity**.

adequate (ad' i kwut) [AD to + EQU equal]—equal to what is required; sufficient. *I was sure my preparation for that exam was adequate.*

equable (ek' wuh bul)—equal at all times; unvarying. *Hawaii has an equable climate, equally pleasant in summer and winter.*

equanimity (ē kwuh nim' uh tē) [EQU equal + ANIM mind]—evenness of mind or temper; composure. *No matter what happened, she always maintained her equanimity.*

equate (i kwāt)—to represent as equal. *It's not possible to equate money and happiness.*

equator (i kwāt' ur)—a line equally distant at all points from the North and South Poles. *The ship sailed across the equator at noon.*

equilateral (ē kwuh lat' ur ul) [EQU equal + LATER side]—having equal sides. *He drew an equilateral triangle on the board.*

equilibrium (ē kwuh lib' rē um) [EQU equal + LIBR balance]—a state of balance. *When the horse swerved, the boy lost his equilibrium and fell off.*

equinox (ē' kwuh noks) [EQU equal + NOX night]—*lit.* equal night; the time of year when the sun crosses the equator and day and night are of equal length. *The spring equinox on March 21 marks the beginning of spring.*

equitable (ek' wuh tuh bul)—reasonable; fair; just. *They achieved an equitable settlement out of court.*

equity (ek' wuh tē)—an ownership right to property. *Because they had paid so little on the mortgage, they had little equity in the house.*

equivalent (i kwiv' u lunt)—equal in value, force, or meaning. *The prize was equivalent to a month's wages.*

equivocal (i kwiv' uh kul) [EQU equal + VOC voice]—*lit.* having equal voices; capable of two interpretations. *Her equivocal reply was so carefully worded that the members of each faction thought she favored them.*

equivocate (i kwiv' uh kāt) [EQU equal + VOC voice]—*lit.* to use equal voices; to make statements with two possible meanings in order to mislead. *The candidate equivocated so much that it was impossible to tell where he stood on any issue.*

ALSO: equalize, equation, equidistant, inadequate, inequality, inequity, iniquity, unequivocal

☐**EXERCISE 1**   Write the appropriate EQU word.

1. It's not always possible to _____ salary and job satisfaction.
2. Because he has so often _____, people are reluctant to
   believe him.
3. Having paid off the mortgage, we now have full _____
   in our house.

4. His _____ in times of crisis was amazing.

5. While trying to get on my bike with my packages, I lost my _____.

6. Florida has a more _____ climate than Maine.

7. After the fall _____, the days get shorter.

8. The shape of the island was roughly that of an _____
   triangle.
9. In giving an _____ answer, he tried to please everyone
   but actually pleased no one.

10. An _____ agreement was finally reached by the contrac-
    tor and the builder.

☐**EXERCISE 2   REVIEW**   Write C in front of each sentence in which all words
are used correctly.

_____   1. Radio and television make it easy to disseminate information.

_____   2. Her excuse was so credible that no one believed her.

_____   3. It usually is possible to correlate vocabulary and success in college.

_____   4. They had a symbiotic relationship, each working better when they
            worked together.

_____   5. A commodious apartment is small but pleasant.

_____   6. A miscreant is an error in a term paper.

_____   7. A bilateral agreement is written in two languages.

_____   8. A coherent speech is orderly and easy to follow.

_____   9. An amphibious animal can live both on land and in the water.

_____ 10. He showed his incredulity by his raised eyebrows.

_____ 11. To circumvent is to open all the windows.

_____ 12. Many children's books have anthropomorphic characters.

_____ 13. Her explanation, full of circumlocutions, never did come to the point.

_____ 14. The speaker's long discourse on dieting was boring.

_____ 15. It was a convivial group that gathered for the holiday celebration.

_____ 16. My friend and I collaborated in designing the poster.

_____ 17. The supervisor went around to circumspect each employee's work.

_____ 18. A companion was originally a person one shared bread with.

_____ 19. The father was an autocrat, with all the rest of the family bowing to his wishes.

_____ 20. A credulous person tends to believe without sufficient evidence.

_____ 21. The tremendous amount of work he did was disproportionate to his small salary.

_____ 22. A consensus is the recording of the population in an area.

_____ 23. She commiserated with me when I lost my job.

_____ 24. His wild tales strain my credulity.

_____ 25. She's a consummate decorator, designing the finest interiors in the city.

_____ 26. The committee decided to convene until after lunch.

_____ 27. Her recurrent absences are giving her a bad reputation.

_____ 28. The dictum of the president left no room for argument.

_____ 29. Our supervisor gets good results without being dictatorial.

_____ 30. The Constitution speaks of the equity of opportunity in our country.

_____ 31. To abdicate is to give up a throne or high office.

_____ 32. His attack of symbiosis was mild, and he soon recovered.

_____ 33. The disease had become pandemic, afflicting many nations.

_____ 34. A biopsy is the examination of tissue taken from a living person whereas an autopsy is the examination of a dead person.

☐**EXERCISE 3 REVIEW** These paragraphs contain eight words you've studied. Can you find all eight? Underline them. Then copy in the space below any words whose meaning you are doubtful about. Look up each of the doubtful words in the Word Index to find the number of the page where the word is explained. When you are sure of the meaning of all the words, read the paragraphs again.

When I first came into this class, I was incredulous at the amount of work assigned. I almost lost my equanimity when I heard that we had to write a daily journal. Soon, though, I realized that the consensus of the class was that the professor is our benefactor.

For a while I was ambivalent, but finally my attitude changed until now it is the antithesis of what it was at first. I now concur with the opinion of the other students and find that I'm adding an incredible number of words to my vocabulary.

☐**EXERCISE 4** Are you adding some words to your WORD LIST at the end of this book? Read your list over occasionally, and try to use a few of your words in conversation.

EU—good, well

If you are in a state of **euphoria,** you feel that life is *good*, that every-thing is going *well*. EU always means *good* or *well*. A **eulogy** is a speech that says *good* things about someone; **euphonious** prose has a pleasant *(good)* sound; and the controversial subject of **euthanasia** is concerned literally with a *good* death, a death for merciful reasons.

Do you ever use **euphemisms**? Look under *euphemism* below and find out.

eulogize (yoo′ luh jīz) [EU good + LOG speech]—*lit.* to give a good speech; to give a speech in praise of. *The man who had started the project was eulogized by all the speakers.*

eulogy (yoo′ luh jē) [EU good + LOG speech]—*lit.* a good speech; spoken or written praise of someone or something, especially praise of a per-son who has recently died. *He gave a moving eulogy at the funeral of his friend.*

euphemism (yoo′ fuh miz um)—the substitution of a mild (good) word in place of a distasteful or unpleasant one. *She spoke in euphemisms, talk-ing of passing on rather than dying, of the departed rather than the dead, and of the underprivileged rather than the poor.*

euphonious (yoo fō′ nē us) [EU good + PHON sound]—having a pleasant (good) sound; harmonious. *I listened to the euphonious sounds of the forest.*

euphony (yoo′ fuh nē) [EU good + PHON sound]—*lit.* good sound; a harmonious succession of words having a pleasing sound. *I like the euphony of the speeches of Martin Luther King, Jr.*

euphoria (yoo fôr′ ē uh)—a feeling of well-being. *After she became engaged, she was in a state of euphoria.*

euthanasia (yoo thuh nā′ zhuh) [EU good + THAN death]—*lit.* a good death; painless putting to death for merciful reasons, as in a terminal illness. *They advocated a law permitting euthanasia for those who are suffering and cannot get well.*

ALSO: eucalyptus, Eugene, eugenics

☐**EXERCISE 1** Write the appropriate EU word.

1. The speaker _____ the soldiers who had died.
2. The sounds coming from the piano practice rooms were not exactly

_____ .

3. Antony's _____ after the death of Julius Caesar is one of the best-known passages in Shakespeare.
4. Instead of speaking of the slums, she always uses the _____ densely populated areas.
5. I was in a state of _____ when I learned that I had been hired.
6. The _____ of the poetry of Robert Frost makes it pleasant to read aloud.
7. Capital punishment and _____ are widely debated issues.

☐**EXERCISE 2 REVIEW** Write C in front of each sentence in which all words are used correctly. Then in each remaining blank, write the word that should have been used.

_____ 1. The anterior legs of an animal are the front legs.

_____ 2. A chronicle is an account of events arranged in order of time.

_____ 3. The doctor prescribed an anecdote for the snakebite.

_____ 4. The results weren't commensurate with the amount of work I put into the project.

_____ 5. On Tuesday morning the two Senate committees held concurrent meetings.

_____ 6. The treasurer failed to disburse the funds in the scholarship account.

_____ 7. An equitable settlement is a fair settlement.

_____ 8. Her office is usually in disarray.

_____ 9. I was incredulous when I heard that she had quit her job.

_____ 10. They didn't condone their child's bad behavior.

_____ 11. Both cars were demolished in the collusion.

_____ 12. Magellan was the first to circumnavigate the globe.

_____ 13. The president would not tolerate any dissent.

☐**EXERCISE 3** List some more euphemisms.

EX, ES, E—out

Our word **escape** means breaking loose from any confinement, but originally it had a more picturesque meaning. In Roman times, perhaps when a jailor was trying to hang on to a prisoner by his cape, the prisoner slipped *out* of his cape and left it in the hands of the jailor: The prisoner had escaped (ES out + CAP cape). He had got "out of his cape" and gone free.

ebullient (i bool' yunt) [E out + BULL to bubble or boil]—bubbling out; overflowing with enthusiasm. *Her ebullient manner made her an entertaining lecturer.*

educate (ej' uh kāt) [E out + DUC to lead]—*lit.* to lead out (draw out) the inborn abilities of a pupil; to develop or train. *I'm trying to educate my puppy.*

efface (i fās') [E out + FAC face]—*lit.* to remove the face of; to wipe out. *Nothing could efface the memory of that storm.*

eject (i jekt') [E out + JECT to throw]—to throw out forcefully. *The landlord ejected the tenants because they did not pay their rent.*

emigrate (em' uh grāt) [E out + MIGRA to move]—to move out of a country (in contrast to immigrate, which means to move into a country). *My ancestors emigrated from Germany.*

emit (ē mit') [E out + MIT to send]—to send out, as a child emits a scream or a factory emits smoke. *The boy emitted a yell as he reached the goal.*

emolument (i mol' yuh munt) [E out + MOL to grind]—originally a miller's fee for grinding (out) grain; now, a payment for services rendered. *Even though she received no emolument, she liked doing the job.*

enervate (en' ur vāt) [E out + NERV nerve]—*lit.* to take out the nerve; to deprive of nerve, force, vigor; to weaken. *She found the hot, humid climate enervating.*

eradicate (i rad' i kāt) [E out + RADIC root]—*lit.* to tear out by the roots; to destroy. *It's difficult to eradicate racial prejudice.*

erase (i rās') [E out + RAS to scrape]—*lit.* to scrape out, as the early Romans scraped off the words they had written on their wax tablets; now, to remove written or recorded material. *The instructor erased the answers on the board.*

escape (is kāp') [ES out + CAP cape]—*lit.* out of one's cape; to break out of confinement. *The convict escaped from prison.*

excavate (ek' skuh vāt) [EX out + CAV hollow]—to hollow out, to dig out and remove. *They were excavating some ancient dinosaur bones.*

exclaim (iks klām') [EX out + CLAM to shout]—*lit.* to shout out; to speak out suddenly. *He exclaimed, "Why shouldn't I go?"*

excoriate (ek skōr' ē āt) [EX out + COR skin]—*lit.* to strip the skin off; to denounce harshly. *The candidate excoriated his opponent, lashing out at him in his public speeches.*

exodus (ek' suh dus) [EX out + OD way]—*lit.* a way out; a departure, usually of a large number of people. *The exodus from the cities to the suburbs has caused much concern.*

exonerate (eg zon' uh rāt) [EX out + ONER burden]—*lit.* to take the burden out; to free from a charge or from guilt. *The jury exonerated him.*

expatiate (ek spā' shē āt) [EX out + SPATIUM space, course]—*lit.* to wander out of the course; to digress; to speak or write at length. *The salesperson expatiated on the value of the product until everyone was bored.*

expatriate (eks pāt' rē ut) [EX out + PATRIA native country]—one who has left one's country or renounced allegiance to it. *She was an expatriate from Germany.*

expel (ik spel') [EX out + PEL to drive]—to drive out. *The child was expelled from school because of repeated absences.*

export (ek spōrt') [EX out + PORT to carry]—to carry out of a country. *Some countries in the tropics export bananas.*

expurgate (eks' pur gāt) [EX out + PURG to clean]—*lit.* to clean out; to take out obscene or objectionable material. *The cast voted to expurgate a shocking scene from the play.*

exterminate (ek stur' muh nāt) [EX out + TERMINUS boundary]—*lit.* to put things out of the boundary; to destroy living things by killing off all individuals. *I'm trying to exterminate these cockroaches.*

Exterminate and eradicate are nearly synonymous. Exterminate means to destroy utterly and is applied to insects or people. Eradicate implies an uprooting and is applied to a disease or a fault or a prejudice.

ALSO: edict, effusive, egregious, eloquent, elucidate, emissary, erupt, eventuate, evoke, exacerbate, excise, exclude, exculpate, expedite, extort

---

□**EXERCISE 1**   Write the appropriate word beginning with EX, ES, E.

1. She found long hikes _____ rather than invigorating.

2. His later years of affluence could not _____ the memory of his early years of privation.

3. The accused was sure the evidence would _____ him.

4. The editor _____ the offensive language from the novel.

5. The kindergarten teacher's lively, _____ personality made the children love her.

6. The volunteers expected no _____ for their services.

7. She _____ at great length about her ailments.

8. The speaker was angry and _____ anyone who disagreed with him.

FID—faith

Did you ever wonder how Fido got his name? He's called Fido because he's *faithful* to his master. The root FID always has something to do with *faith*. **Fidelity** means *faith*fulness, and **infidelity** means un*faith*fulness. If you are **confident,** you have *faith* in yourself, but if you are **diffident** [DI not + FID faith], you don't have *faith* in yourself; you are shy.

Sometimes, as in **confide** and several other words below, CON is used merely as an intensive, giving more emphasis to the root that follows.

bona fide (bō' nuh fīd) [BON good + FID faith]—*lit.* in good faith; genuine. *They made a bona fide offer on the house. The museum has a bona fide painting by Gauguin.*

confidant (kahn' fuh dant) [CON (intensive) + FID faith]—*lit.* a person one has faith in; a person one confides in. *Her dad had been her confidant for years.*

confide (kun fīd') [CON (intensive) + FID faith]—to show faith by sharing secrets. *I'd never confide in such a gossip.*

confident (kahn' fud unt) [CON (intensive) + FID faith]—having faith in oneself, self-assured. *My brother was confident as he walked onto the stage.*

confidential (kahn fuh den' chul) [CON (intensive) + FID faith]—marked by intimacy or willingness to confide. *What I am going to tell you is confidential.*

diffident (dif' uh dunt) [DIF not + FID faith]—not having faith in oneself; shy. *The youngster was diffident about speaking in public.*

fidelity (fi del' uh tē)—faithfulness. *His fidelity to the party platform was questionable.*

infidel (in' fuh dul) [IN not + FID faith]—*lit.* not faithful; a person who does not believe in a particular religion. *The Muslims were in conflict with the infidels.*

infidelity (in fuh del' uh tē) [IN not + FID faith]—unfaithfulness, especially in marriage. *No one had ever accused him of infidelity.*

perfidious (per fid' ē us) [PER through + FID faith]—deceiving through a pretense of faith; treacherous. *Her perfidious actions branded her as someone not to be trusted.*

ALSO: affidavit, confidence, perfidy

☐**EXERCISE 1**   Write the appropriate FID word.

1. He owned a _____ Model T Ford.

2. Even a _____ person will enjoy choral reading because one loses one's shyness in the group.

3. His _____ attempts to undermine the work of his own committee were shocking.

4. Anyone not following the state religion was called an _____.

5. You can be sure of his _____; he would never be unfaithful.

6. She needed a _____ with whom she could discuss her problems.

☐**EXERCISE 2   REVIEW**   Write a sentence of your own for each word. You may use a sentence from a preceding page if you can remember it without looking back.

1. ambidextrous

2. asymmetrical

3. ambivalent

4. credulous

5. automaton

6. bilingual

7. anachronism

GEN—birth, race, kind

In ancient mythology, when a child was born, a guardian spirit or **genius** (so named because it appeared at *birth*) was appointed to guide the person throughout life. Today, although we no longer believe we are given a guiding genius at birth, still we may have within us from *birth* a genius for something such as math or painting. Thus the ancient guiding genius has now become an exceptional intellectual or creative ability.

GEN has four main meanings.

1. First of all, **GEN** means *birth*—not only the *birth* of people but also the *birth* of things (an engine **generates** or gives *birth* to electricity) and the *birth* of ideas (angry words **engender** or give *birth* to hate whereas kind words engender love).

engender (in jen' dur)—*lit.* to give birth to; to develop; to bring forth, as ideas or feelings. *His handling of the problem engendered the respect of his fellow workers.*

generate (jen' uh rāt)—*lit.* to give birth to; to produce, as an engine generates power. *By turning a windmill, the wind can generate electricity.*

generation (jen uh rā' shun)—all the people born at about the same time. *They were trying to understand the younger generation.*

genesis (jen' uh sis)—the birth or coming into being of anything; origin; creation. *His many childhood pets were the genesis of his interest in zoology.*

genius (jēn' yus)—in ancient mythology, a guardian spirit appointed at birth to guide a person; now, an exceptional intellectual or creative ability. *She's a genius at painting.*

hydrogen (hī' druh jun) [HYDR water + GEN birth]—a gas so called because it generates (gives birth to) water by its combustion. *Hydrogen gas was used in the first balloons to carry men into the sky.*

ingenious (in jēn' yus) [IN in + GEN birth]—*lit.* having inborn talent; clever at contriving. *It took an ingenious architect to design a house for such a small lot.*

ingenuous (in jen' yoo us) [IN in + GEN birth]—*lit.* freeborn, honest; showing innocent or childlike simplicity or gullibility. *She was completely ingenuous, never questioning anything she was told.*

2. **GEN** also indicates noble or good *birth* or breeding.

generous—liberal in giving as a person of noble birth would be
genial—having a friendly and kindly manner
genteel—having an aristocratic quality; refined in manner
gentility—the condition of being genteel
gentleman—a man of noble or gentle birth; a polite, considerate man
gentry—people of gentle birth or high social position

3. **GEN** also means *race*. If you are interested in your family history, you are interested in **genealogy,** the study of the ancestors of a family.

gene (jēn)—an element of the germ plasm that transmits characteristics of the parents, and hence of the race, to the child. *Information stored in the genes determines an individual's eventual height.*

genealogy (jē nē al' uh jē) [GEN race + -LOGY study of]—*lit.* the study of race; the study of family descent. *After seeing "Roots," many people became interested in genealogy.*

genetics (juh net' iks)—the science of heredity. *Fruit flies are often used in experiments in genetics because they reproduce so quickly.*

genocide (jen' uh sīd) [GEN race + CID to kill]—the systematic, planned killing of a racial, political, or cultural group. *Genocide is unthinkable in any civilized society.*

progenitor (prō jen' uh tur) [PRO forth + GEN birth]—a direct ancestor. *Their zeal for social reform could be traced to their progenitor.*

progeny (proj' uh nē) [PRO forth + GEN birth]—children or descendants. *His progeny inherited his amibition.*

4. **GEN** also means a category or *kind*.

generic (juh ner' ik)—general kind; commonly available; not protected by a trademark, as generic drugs. *She usually economizes by buying generic cereals instead of name brands.*

genre (zhahn' ruh)—a particular kind or category of literature or art. *He hadn't limited his reading to a single genre but had delved into poetry, the short story, and the novel.*

ALSO: congenital, cryptogenic, degenerate, eugenics, general, heterogeneous, homogeneous, homogenize, pathogenic, primogeniture

---

☐**EXERCISE 1**   Write the appropriate GEN word.

1. The Montgomery bus boycott was the _____ of the civil rights movement.

2. I've been recording all the dates I can find for our family_____.

3. His friendliness _____ good feeling in the company.

4. Their _____ came over from Germany a century ago.

5. She chose the short story as her _____ for study.

6. He had so many grandchildren that he had lost count of all his _____.

7. Her _____ answers showed her childlike innocence.

GRAPH, GRAM—to write

We don't usually think of **geography** as having anything to do with writing, but it is made up of GEO, *earth,* and GRAPH, to *write,* and is actually a *writing* about the surface of the earth. Note how each of the following words has something to do with *writing.*

autograph (aw' tuh graf) [AUTO self + GRAPH to write]—*lit.* the writing of oneself; one's signature. *The author autographed his book for me.*

calligraphy (kuh lig' ruh fē) [CALLI beautiful + GRAPH to write]—the art of fine handwriting. *She copied a favorite poem in beautiful calligraphy and had it framed.*

cardiogram (kahr' dē uh gram) [CARD heart + GRAM to write]—a written tracing showing the contractions of the heart. *The cardiogram showed a few extra heartbeats.*

choreography (kōr ē og' ruh fē) [CHOR dance + GRAPH to write]—*lit.* the writing of a story in dance; the creating and arranging of dance movements, especially ballet. *The director of the opera also did the choreography.*

diagram (dī' uh gram) [DIA through + GRAM to write]—*lit.* a writing to show through something, to make it plain; a drawing that explains something. *We were given a diagram of the route we were to take.*

epigram (ep' uh gram) [EPI on + GRAM to write]—*lit.* a writing on a subject; any short, witty saying. *She liked to quote the epigram "Success is getting what you want; happiness is wanting what you get."*

geography (jē og' ruh fē) [GEO earth + GRAPH to write]—*lit.* a writing about the earth; a science dealing with the earth and its life. *Geography was my favorite subject in grade school.*

graffiti (gra fē' tē)—crude drawings or writings scratched on public walls. *Getting rid of graffiti on the subway walls was the next civic project.*

graphic (graf' ik)—full of vivid details. *The author gave a graphic description of the earthquake.*

graphite (graf' īt)—a soft, black, lustrous form of carbon found in nature and used for lead in pencils (for writing). *Graphite has many other uses besides supplying the lead for pencils.*

hologram (hō' luh gram) [HOLO whole + GRAM to write]—a three-dimensional photograph made using lasers. *The cover of the* National Geographic *for December 1988 was a hologram.*

monogram (mon' uh gram) [MONO one + GRAM to write]—two or more letters entwined (written) into one design. *On each towel she embroidered a monogram.*

monograph (mon' uh graf) [MONO one + GRAPH to write]—a book written about one specific subject. *She published a monograph about the biblical references in Browning's poems.*

program (prō' gram) [PRO before + GRAM to write]—*lit.* a writing beforehand; a listing of things to follow; a printed announcement of events; in computer science, a sequential set of commands to be followed by a computer. *I was the first one on the program.*

seismograph (sīz' muh graf) [SEISMOS earthquake + GRAPH to write]— an instrument for recording (writing) the intensity and duration of an earthquake. *The seismograph recorded an earthquake that registered 7 on the Richter scale.*

stenographer (stuh nahg' ruh fur) [STEN narrow + GRAPH to write]—*lit.* one who uses narrow or small writing (shorthand); a person who takes dictation in shorthand. *I wish I had a stenographer to help me write my compositions.*

topography (tuh pahg' ruh fē) [TOP place + GRAPH to write]—a detailed drawing (writing) on a map of the surface features of a region (place) showing their relative positions and elevations. *Before venturing into the canyon, the hikers studied its topography.*

ALSO: autobiography, bibliography, biography, cryptography, demographic, lithography, orthography, phonograph, photography, telegram, telegraph

---

□**EXERCISE 1** Write the appropriate GRAPH, GRAM word.

1. To make her writing true to life, she used many _____ details.

2. Her stationery was decorated with her _____.

3. The _____ of the Tchaikovsky ballet was entirely new.

4. A study of the _____ of the region showed many caves and hills.

5. The heart specialist explained to the patient the meaning of the jiggles on

   the _____.

6. The fence around the construction was covered with amusing _____.

7. The professor wrote a _____ about his research on cloning.

8. My aunt kept quoting the _____ "A place for everything, and everything in its place."

□**EXERCISE 2** List as many epigrams as you can think of. Remember those your parents have used: "Haste makes waste," "A penny saved is a penny earned.". . .

LOG—speech, word

Words containing the root LOG have to do with *speech*. A **monologue** is a *speech* by one person. A **dialogue** is *speech* between two or more people. A **prologue** is a *speech* before a play, and an **epilogue** is a *speech* after it. (Note that all of these words can also be spelled without the *ue* ending.)

analogous (uh nal' uh gus) [ANA according to + LOG speech, reason]—similar in some ways but not in others. *The wings of a bird and those of an airplane are analogous, having a similar function but a different origin and structure.*

analogy (uh nal' uh jē) [ANA according to + LOG speech, reason]—resemblance in some particulars between things otherwise unlike. *To get his point across, the professor used the following analogy: cutting classes is like paying for a hamburger and then walking away without eating it.*

apology (a pol' uh jē) [APO away + LOG speech]—*lit.* a speaking away; a speech expressing regret for a fault or offense. *I offered him an apology.*

dialogue (dī' uh log) [DIA between + LOG speech]—speech between two or more people; a conversational passage in a play or narrative. *After a long dialogue, we finally resolved our difficulties.*

doxology (dok sol' uh jē) [DOX praise + LOG speech]—a hymn or expression of praise to God. *The best-known doxology is the one sung in Protestant churches, beginning "Praise God from whom all blessings flow."*

epilogue (ep' uh log) [EPI on + LOG speech]—a speech directed to the audience at the conclusion of a play. *Shakespeare's plays often end with an epilogue spoken by one of the characters.*

monologue (mon' uh log) [MONO one + LOG speech]—a speech by one person; a soliloquy. *The monologue beginning "Is this a dagger which I see before me?" helps reveal Macbeth's character.*

prologue (prō' log) [PRO before + LOG speech]—a speech before a play. Romeo and Juliet *begins with a prologue that summarizes the story for the audience.* Also, any introductory event. *The fancy appetizers were the prologue to an excellent dinner.*

travelogue (trav' uh log) [TRAVEL journey + LOG speech]—a speech or film about travel. *We heard a travelogue about Greenland.*

ALSO: analog, decalogue, eulogy, logic

□**EXERCISE 1** Write the appropriate LOG word.

1. The _____ at the end of the play pointed out the moral.
2. It was hard to get a word in because his conversation was really a

_____.

3. Her first complaint was just a _____ to what was to come.

4. The lecturer made each point clear by using an _____.

5. The witty _____ between the characters made *The Taming of the Shrew* famous.

6. Reading a book is _____ to dropping chemicals into a test tube; there should be a reaction.

☐**EXERCISE 2   REVIEW**   Write C in front of each sentence in which all words are used correctly. Then in each remaining blank, write the word that should have been used.

_____ 1. Discomfited and disconcerted both mean to be upset about something.

_____ 2. The speaker's talk was full of humorous antidotes.

_____ 3. Euphoria is a feeling of well-being.

_____ 4. A genre is a particular category of literature or art.

_____ 5. The play begins with the two actors on the stage presenting a monologue.

_____ 6. An epigram is a short, witty saying.

_____ 7. Choreography is the arranging of dance movements.

_____ 8. The beagle Snoopy in "Peanuts" is an anthropomorphic character.

_____ 9. She's a good switch hitter because she's ambidextrous.

_____ 10. The doctor wrote the prescription for a generic rather than a brand name drug to save the patient money.

_____ 11. Her father's incredulity was obvious as he listened to her excuses.

_____ 12. My cousin has invented an ingenuous device for keeping coat hangers apart.

_____ 13. The term rest room is a euphemism.

_____ 14. A misanthrope aids various humanitarian causes.

☐**EXERCISE 3**   A dull subject can often be made more vivid and interesting by using an analogy. Note how effectively an analogy is used in this sentence from *Time*: *Like a pilot bailing out of a flaming aircraft and then waiting terror-stricken to see if his parachute will open, American businesspeople and economists hung impatiently last week trying to see how deep the recession would go.*

-LOGY—study of

-LOGY at the end of a word usually means *study of.* **Biology** [BIO life] is the *study of* plant and animal life. **Geology** [GEO earth] is the *study of* the history of the earth, especially as recorded in rocks. **Etymology** [ETYM true] is the *study of* the origin (true meaning) and development of words. In this book you are getting an introduction to etymology.

Almost all such words have O in front of the -LOGY so that the ending is -OLOGY. But two words have A in front of the -LOGY— genealogy and mineralogy.

archeology (ahr kē ol′ uh jē) [ARCH ancient + -LOGY study of]—the study of ancient cultures based on artifacts and other remains. *Egypt is a good place to study archeology because the monuments and artifacts are well preserved.*

astrology (uh strol′ uh jē) [ASTR star + -LOGY study of]—a pseudoscience claiming to foretell the future by a study of the stars. *To try to foresee her future, she consulted a book on astrology.*

ecology (ē kol′ uh jē) [ECO home + -LOGY study of]—the study of the relationship between organisms and their environment (home). *The ecology of the region showed that the number of wild animals had decreased as a result of lumbering.*

embryology (em brē ol′ uh jē)—the study of the formation and development of embryos. *The science of embryology has determined the exact times when various parts of an embryo develop.*

entomology (en tuh mol′ uh jē) [EN in + TOM to cut + -LOGY study of]— the study of insects (whose bodies are "cut" in three segments). *The entomology class was studying grasshoppers.*

etymology (et uh mol′ uh jē) [ETYM true + -LOGY study of]—the study of the origin (true meaning) and development of words. *From his study of etymology, he learned many interesting word histories.*

geology (jē ol′ uh jē) [GEO earth + -LOGY study of]—the study of the history of the earth, especially as recorded in rocks. *The geology of the Grand Canyon shows various periods in the earth's development.*

meteorology (mē tē uh rol′ uh jē) [METEORA things in the air + -LOGY study of]—the study of the atmosphere, especially weather and weather conditions. *The Bureau of Meteorology is recording slight changes in climate from year to year.*

ornithology (awr nuh thol′ uh jē) [ORNITH bird + -LOGY study of]—the branch of zoology dealing with birds. *Because he was interested in ornithology, he made recordings of bird songs.*

psychology (sī kol′ uh jē) [PSYCH mind + -LOGY study of]—the study of mental processes and behavior. *His study of psychology helped him understand himself.*

ALSO: anthropology, bacteriology, biology, chronology, dermatology, genealogy, gynecology, mineralogy, morphology, paleontology, pathology, physiology, technology, theology, zoology

□**EXERCISE 1**   What science makes a study of the following?

1. the human mind   _____

2. weather conditions   _____

3. the origin and development of words   _____

4. the history of the earth as recorded in rocks   _____

5. ancient cultures based on their artifacts
   and monuments   _____

6. insects   _____

7. birds   _____

8. embryos   _____

9. the relationship of organisms to their
   environment   _____

□**EXERCISE 2**   In this book you have been studying etymology. List three words—and the etymology of each—that you have found most interesting.

□**EXERCISE 3**   Add a few more words to your WORD LIST on a blank page at the end of the book. Record words that you hope to use in conversation or in writing.

LOQU, LOC—to speak

A **soliloquy** [SOL alone + LOQU to speak] is a *speech* given by an actor, alone on the stage, to reveal private thoughts and emotions. The most famous soliloquy, of course, is Hamlet's "To be or not to be," when Hamlet reveals his feelings to the audience. Another soliloquy from a Shakespearean play is the opening speech of *Richard III,* "Now is the winter of our discontent. . . ."

colloquial (kuh lō′ kwē ul) [COL together + LOQU to speak]—like the language used when people speak together informally; informal or conversational. *"Passing the buck" is a colloquial expression for "shifting responsibility."*

colloquium (kuh lō′ kwē um) [COL together + LOQU to speak]—*lit.* a speaking together; an academic seminar on some field of study, led by several experts. *They attended the colloquium on Hemingway.*

eloquent (el′ uh kwunt) [E out + LOQU to speak]—*lit.* speaking out; fluent; persuasive. *The audience was moved by the eloquent speaker.*

grandiloquent (gran dil′ uh kwunt) [GRAND grand + LOQU to speak]—marked by a lofty, extravagantly colorful style. *The Duke tries to impress Huckleberry Finn with his grandiloquent speech.*

loquacious (lō kwā′ shus)—talkative. *It was my luck to get a loquacious partner at bridge.*

soliloquy (suh lil′ uh kwē) [SOL alone + LOQU to speak]—a speaking alone to oneself, as in a drama; a monologue. *The soliloquy is used less frequently in modern drama than in earlier plays.*

ventriloquist (ven tril′ uh kwist) [VENTR stomach + LOQU to speak]—*lit.* one who speaks from the stomach; one who speaks so that the sounds seem to come from somewhere other than the speaker's mouth. *The ventriloquist was able to speak without moving his lips while manipulating the lower jaw of the puppet on his lap.*

ALSO: circumlocution, colloquy, elocution, eloquence, interlocutor, loquacity, obloquy

---

☐**EXERCISE 1** Write the appropriate LOQU, LOC word.

1. She was so _____ that no one else had a chance to say anything.

2. He uses a _____ rather than a formal style of writing.

3. The lecturer hoped his _____ style of speaking, with big words and impressive gestures, would make up for his lack of ideas.

4. A dramatist may reveal a character's feelings to the audience through a

_____.

5. The man with the puppet on his knee was a _____.

6. Six professors took part in the _____ on hazardous waste.

☐**EXERCISE 2 REVIEW** Write C in front of each sentence in which all words are used correctly.

_____ 1. Radio was the precursor of television.

_____ 2. Maintaining one's equanimity is maintaining one's poise and composure.

_____ 3. The suit for divorce accused him of gentility.

_____ 4. To feel some compunction about something you have done is to feel a slight regret about it.

_____ 5. Meteorology has now made weather prediction more accurate.

_____ 6. Always interested in butterflies, she decided to major in entomology.

_____ 7. They were repainting the fence to get rid of the objectionable graffiti.

_____ 8. A disconsolate person tries to comfort others.

_____ 9. A confidant is a person one confides in.

_____ 10. Through the study of genetics, scientists are making discoveries about heredity.

_____ 11. They own a bona fide Seth Thomas clock dating from 1850.

_____ 12. Diffident means various kinds.

☐**EXERCISE 3** Write some pairs of sentences, the first sentence in colloquial English and the second in formal English.

1.

1.

2.

2.

3.

3.

MAL—bad

In the medieval calendar, two days in each month were marked as *dies mali* (evil days)—January 1 and 25, February 4 and 26, March 1 and 28, April 10 and 20, May 3 and 25, June 10 and 16, July 13 and 22, August 1 and 30, September 3 and 21, October 3 and 22, November 5 and 28, and December 7 and 22. Any enterprise begun on one of these *bad days* was certain to end in failure. Our word **dismal** comes from *dies mali*, but today a dismal day is merely gloomy or depressing.

Was he really ill when he stayed at home from work during the week of the World Series, or was he just malingering? **Malinger** originally meant to be in *bad* health, but, as with many words, it has changed over the years and now means to pretend to be ill in order to avoid duty or work. If you stay home from work pretending to be ill, you're malingering. If you claim you have a bad back when the walks need shoveling, if you develop a headache when you're supposed to go to a boring meeting, if you are too weary after dinner to help with the dishes—you could be malingering.

A number of words beginning with MAL are easy to understand because MAL simply gives the word a "bad" meaning.

malnutrition is bad nutrition
maltreated means badly treated
maladjusted means badly adjusted to the circumstances of one's life
malfunction means to function badly, as an engine malfunctions
malpractice means improper treatment of a patient by a physician

maladroit (mal uh droit′)—not adroit; not skillful; awkward; clumsy. *The new supervisor was maladroit in dealing with the employees.*

malady (mal′ uh dē)—*lit.* a bad condition; a disease. *Science has reduced the number of incurable maladies.*

malaise (mal āz′) [MAL bad + AISE ease]—a vague feeling of illness or depression. *As she was preparing for the interview, a slight malaise came over her.*

malaproprism (mal′ uh prop iz uhm)—*lit.* badly appropriate; not appropriate; a ludicrous misuse of a word that sounds somewhat like the word intended. (From Sheridan's play *The Rivals* in which Mrs. Malaprop misuses words, as when she speaks of a shrewd awakening instead of a rude awakening.) *Archie Bunker made television viewers of the seventies laugh at his malapropisms, as when he said, "The donor may wish to remain unanimous."*

malaria (muh ler′ ē uh) [MAL bad + AER air]—a disease once thought to be caused by bad air from the swamps. *Malaria is often contracted in the tropics.*

malcontent (mal' kun tent)—*lit.* one who is badly contented; a discontented or rebellious person. *He was a born malcontent, always complaining.*

malediction (mal uh dik' shun) [MAL bad + DICT to speak]—a curse (opposite of benediction). *The leader of the cult pronounced a malediction upon all those who did not follow him.*

malevolent (muh lev' uh lunt) [MAL bad + VOL to wish]—wishing evil toward others. *The defendant cast a malevolent glance toward his accuser.*

malfeasance (mal fē'zuns) [MAL bad + FAC to do]—wrongdoing, especially by a public official. *The mayor was accused of malfeasance in his distribution of public funds.*

malice (mal' is)—active bad feeling or ill will. *The past president felt no malice toward the candidate who defeated him.*

malicious (muh lish' us)—intentionally bad or harmful. *She refused to listen to malicious gossip.*

malign (muh līn')–to speak evil of; to slander. *In the political debate his opponent maligned him.*

malignant (muh lig' nunt)—bad or harmful; likely to cause death. *The biopsy revealed that the growth was not malignant.*

malinger (muh ling' gur)—to pretend to be in bad health to get out of work. *Since his headaches always occurred just at schooltime, we thought he was malingering.*

ALSO: malefactor, malformed, malocclusion, malodorous

□**EXERCISE 1**   Write the appropriate MAL word.

1. Having used up his sick leave, he was no longer tempted to _____.

2. He suffered from one _____ after another.

3. Although the working conditions were ideal, the _____ always found something to complain about.

4. Her _____ gossip about her opponent was uncalled-for.

5. They had feared the tumor was _____, but it was benign.

6. She tried to _____ her fellow workers, saying untrue things about them.

7. Understandably, they felt some _____ toward her.

8. The villagers trembled when they heard the _____ that the witch doctor pronounced.

9. A charge of _____ was brought against the party boss because of his misuse of party funds.

10. He avoided the _____ stare of his opponent.

11. As the time for his speech approached, his feeling of _____
increased.
12. Her bungling way of handling the problem was _____
to say the least.
13. In her attempt to use big words, she often used _____.

☐**EXERCISE 2**　In *The Rivals* Mrs. Malaprop says that Lydia is as headstrong as
an allegory on the banks of the Nile. What word did she intend to use? List some
malapropisms you have heard.

☐**EXERCISE 3　REVIEW**　Write C in front of each sentence in which all words
are used correctly. Then in each remaining blank, write the word that should have
been used.

_____ 1. I find jogging enervating and always feel exhausted afterward.

_____ 2. Her perfidious dealings were shocking because she had
been such a trusted employee.

_____ 3. I give little credence to the testimony of such an untrustworthy witness.

_____ 4. In his study of his genealogy, he discovered that his ancestors had once lived in Holland.

_____ 5. Concern about what is happening to our environment has led
to a new interest in ecology.

_____ 6. The suit against him charged him with fidelity to the company
he worked for.

_____ 7. After losing her job, she was disconsolate.

_____ 8. Trying to cross the little stream on a log, I lost my equilibrium.

☐EXERCISE 4 REVIEW This paragraph contains 12 words you have studied. Are you sure of the meaning of all of them? Copy any that you aren't sure of in the space below. Then turn to the Word Index to find the number of the page where each word is explained. After you are sure of the meaning of each word, reread the paragraph to see how gratifying it is to read with no questions about word meaning.

Our political <u>conventions</u> are a <u>graphic</u> example of our <u>democracy</u> at work. Before the convention, the platform <u>committee</u> must reach a <u>consensus</u> on a platform that will be <u>ambiguous</u> enough to avoid offending anyone, yet strong enough to <u>engender</u> support. At the convention itself, <u>grandiloquent</u> speeches <u>eulogize</u> the candidates and <u>malign</u> the opposition. Finally, although the actual choice of a candidate is often an <u>anticlimax</u> because the outcome has been known all along, the convention does answer the <u>perennial</u> human question, "Who shall lead?"

☐EXERCISE 5 In your journal write a sentence listing a few new words that you're sure you're going to use in conversation.

METER, METR—measure

Although for years Americans have used the root METER in such words as **thermometer, barometer, speedometer,** and **odometer,** we are dragging our feet in adopting the **metric system.** Only two other countries in the world don't use metric: Liberia and Myanmar (formerly called Burma). But now, with many states requiring metric instruction in the schools, perhaps we will eventually go along with the rest of the metric world.

barometer (bu rahm′ uh tur) [BAR pressure + METER measure]—an instrument for measuring atmospheric pressure and hence for assisting in predicting probable weather changes. *Since the barometer reading is falling, I'm afraid we may have a storm.*

geometry (jē ahm′ uh trē) [GEO earth + METR measure]—*lit.* earth measuring; originally, the system of measuring distances on earth through the use of angles; now, a branch of mathematics that deals with points, lines, planes, and solids. *I find geometry easier than algebra.*

kilometer (kuh lom′ uh tur) [KILO thousand + METER measure]—1,000 meters; approximately 0.62 mile. *In Canada the speed limits are posted in kilometers.*

metric system (me′ trik)—a decimal system of weights and measures based on the meter as a unit length and the kilogram as a unit mass. *The metric system is used almost worldwide.*

metronome (met′ ruh nōm) [METR measure + NOM law]—a clocklike instrument for measuring the exact time (law) in music by a regularly repeated tick. *Practicing the piano with a metronome helped her keep perfect time.*

odometer (ō dom′ uh tur) [OD road + METER measure]—*lit.* a road measure; an instrument for measuring the distance traveled by a vehicle. *His policy was to trade in his car when the odometer registered 50,000 miles.*

parameter (puh ram′ uh tar) [PARA beside + METER measure]—a fixed limit or boundary. *Stay within the parameters of the present budget.*

pedometer (pi dom′ uh tur) [PED foot + METER measure]—an instrument that measures the distance walked by recording the number of steps taken. *To make sure she walked two miles a day, she took a pedometer with her.*

perimeter (puh rim′ uh tur) [PERI around + METER measure]—the boundary around an area. *An old rail fence ran along the perimeter of his farm.*

symmetrical (si met′ ri kul) [SYM together + METR measure]—*lit.* measured together; having both sides exactly alike. *He made a symmetrical flower arrangement for the center of the table.*

tachometer (ta kahm' uh tur) [TACH speed + METER measure]—an instrument used to measure the speed of a revolving shaft in revolutions per minute. *My "tach" indicated that my engine was going too fast.*

trigonometry (trig uh nom' uh trē) [TRI three + GON angle + METR measure]—the branch of mathematics that deals with the relations between the sides and angles of triangles and the calculations based on these. *Her knowledge of trigonometry was of value in her surveying job.*

ALSO: asymmetrical, centimeter, chronometer, diameter, isometric, micrometer, pentameter, telemetry, thermometer

---

☐**EXERCISE 1** What word containing the root METER, METR names or describes the following?

1. the boundary around an area _____

2. an instrument that measures atmospheric pressure _____

3. an instrument for measuring the distance traveled by a vehicle _____

4. approximately 0.62 mile _____
5. an instrument that measures time in music by a regularly repeated tick

_____

6. an instrument that measures the distance walked by recording the number of

steps taken _____

7. having both sides exactly alike _____
8. an instrument used to measure the revolutions per minute of a revolving shaft

_____

☐**EXERCISE 2 REVIEW** Underline the appropriate word.

1. He spent a (disproportionate, diverse) amount of time on the first part of the book.
2. The students were bored as the professor (expatiated, equivocated) about his pet theory.
3. Instead of reading my report carefully, the supervisor gave it only a (dictatorial, cursory) glance.
4. After consulting many old records, she learned what country her father's (progenitors, progeny) had come from.

MIT, MIS, MISS—to send

The MIT, MIS, MISS root has to do with sending. A **mission** is a task that one is *sent* to do. A **missionary** is someone *sent* out to do religious work. A **message** is a communication *sent* to someone, and the person who carries the message is a **messenger**.

dismiss (dis mis′) [DIS away + MISS to send]—to send away. *The professor dismissed the class.*

emissary (em′ uh ser ē) [E out + MISS to send]—a person sent out on a specific mission. *The government sent an emissary to look into the matter.*

intermittent (in tur mit′ unt) [INTER between + MIT to send]—*lit.* sent between intervals; stopping and starting at intervals. *The intermittent rain didn't prevent them from enjoying the game.*

missile (mis′ ul) [MISS to send]—a weapon that is fired or otherwise sent toward a target. *They fired the missile toward the enemy.*

missive (mis′ iv)—a letter or message that is sent. *A missive from the president directed their next move.*

omit (ō mit′) [OB away + MIT to send]—*lit.* to send away; to leave out. *You'd better omit that unnecessary paragraph.*

permit (pur mit′) [PER through + MIT to send]—*lit.* to send through; to allow. *The tutor won't permit unnecessary talking.*

premise (prem′ is) [PRE before + MIS to send]—*lit.* a statement sent before; an initial statement that is assumed to be true and upon which an argument is based. *His argument failed because he started with a false premise.*

promise (prahm′ us) [PRO forth + MIS to send]—*lit.* to send forth; to indicate what may be expected. *I promise to help you.*

transmission (trans mish′ un) [TRANS across + MISS to send]—a device that sends (across) power from the engine of an automobile to the wheels. *The transmission in his car is giving him trouble.* Also, the act of transmitting. *Their office requested immediate transmission of the document.*

transmit (trans mit′) [TRANS across + MIT to send]—to send (across) from one place or person to another. *The lawyer will transmit the document to his client.*

ALSO: admit, commission, commit, commitment, committee, demise, emit, intermission, omission, remiss, remission, remit, submit

☐**EXERCISE 1 REVIEW** Write C in front of each sentence in which all words are used correctly. You're on your own now. No answers are provided at the back of the book for this exercise.

_____ 1. Graphic writing uses vivid details.

_____ 2. An infidel is a Cuban revolutionary.

_____ 3. Ornithology is the study of birds.

_____ 4. They have diverse interests; he likes music and she likes sports.

_____ 5. Equilateral describes measurements along the equator.

_____ 6. My progenitors on my mother's side came from Germany.

_____ 7. A loquacious person talks too much.

_____ 8. A prologue comes at the beginning of a play and an epilogue at the end.

_____ 9. It was once thought that malaria was caused by bad air.

_____ 10. Archeology is the study of the remains of ancient civilizations.

_____ 11. Malaise is a vague feeling of illness or depression.

_____ 12. Malingering means lingering too long over meals.

_____ 13. To eradicate is literally to tear out by the roots.

_____ 14. Your pedometer tells you how far you have driven.

_____ 15. In Shakespearean plays one actor often speaks alone in a soliloquy.

_____ 16. She noted by her odometer that she was going over 55.

_____ 17. A malcontent is chronically unhappy.

_____ 18. To emit something is to leave it out.

_____ 19. An equivocal answer could be interpreted two ways.

_____ 20. A climate with little change all year is called equable.

_____ 21. He was afraid to use big words for fear he'd use a malapropism.

_____ 22. The final location of the factory will depend on demographic data.

_____ 23. A colloquium was held to discuss the diseases now found in developing nations.

_____ 24. The judge had a benign attitude toward first offenders.

_____ 25. Equinox refers to an Eskimo dwelling.

MONO—one

There are two roots meaning *one*—UNI (as in **unanimous, unify, unison**) and MONO. MONO is found is such words as **monoplane** (having only *one* pair of wings), **monarchy** (having *one* ruler), and **monotheism** (belief in *one* God). Two words we don't usually think of as containing MONO are monk and monastery. A **monk** was originally *one* religious man living alone, and a **monastery** was a dwelling place for monks living in seclusion from the world.

monarchy (mahn′ ahr kē) [MONO one + ARCH ruler]—a government with one hereditary ruler. *At the end of the war the monarchy became a democracy.*

monastery (mahn′ uh ster ē)—a dwelling place for monks living secluded from the world. *The monastery was high in the mountains.*

monk (munk)—originally, one religious man living alone; now, a member of a religious brotherhood living in a monastery. *The monks formed a school for the disabled.*

monocle (mon′ uh kul) [MONO one + OCUL eye]—an eyeglass for one eye. *The English gentleman looked at us through his monocle.*

monogamy (muh nog′ uh mē) [MONO one + GAM marriage]—marriage to only one person at a time. *Monogamy is practiced in most countries today.*

monolith (mon′ uh lith) [MONO one + LITH stone]—one single large piece of stone, as a monument or a statue. *The monoliths at Stonehenge were transported from a great distance in prehistoric times.*

monolithic (mon uh lith′ ik) [MONO one + LITH stone]—like one single stone, hence solid, massive, and uniform. *The corporation had become monolithic with one strong central organization.*

monopoly (muh nahp′ uh lē) [MONO one + POLY to sell]—exclusive control by one group of a commodity or service. *The student store had a monopoly on selling college sweatshirts.*

monosyllable (mon′ uh sil uh bul)—a word of one syllable. *She thought she had to speak to the child in monosyllables.*

monotheism (mon′ uh thē iz um) [MONO one + THE god]—the belief that there is only one God. *Unlike their neighbors, the early Hebrews held to monotheism.*

monotone (mon′ uh tōn) [MONO one + TON tone]—having one tone; lack of variety in tone. *Because the professor always spoke in a monotone, his students fell asleep.*

monotonous (muh not′ n us) [MONO one + TON tone]—*lit.* one tone; having no variation. *Her constant complaints became monotonous.*

ALSO: monochromatic, monogamist, monogram, monograph, monologue, mononucleosis, monoplane, monopolize, monorail, monotony

☐**EXERCISE 1** Write the appropriate MONO word.

1. At least it's easy to tell where the accent falls in a _____.

2. _____ is the central belief of Christians, Jews, and Muslims.

3. Her speeches are boring because she speaks in a _____.

4. The island tribe practiced _____ and had strong taboos against marital infidelity.

5. The company was _____, with a reputation for uniform policy in all its branches.

6. In Tonga we saw huge _____ that had been set up in prehistoric times.

☐**EXERCISE 2   REVIEW**   Write C in front of each sentence in which all words are used correctly.

_____ 1. Many people think there should be a law permitting euthanasia.

_____ 2. After I dismantled my typewriter, I couldn't put it back together again.

_____ 3. Her towels were embroidered with her monogram.

_____ 4. The new plastic heart in his body ticked like a metronome.

_____ 5. "All leaves are green" would be a false premise.

_____ 6. They studied a map showing the topography of the area they were entering.

_____ 7. A cardiogram is a short, witty saying.

_____ 8. The governor issued an edict forbidding government workers to strike.

_____ 9. Intermittent showers in Hawaii are called liquid sunshine.

_____ 10. The jury exonerated him, and he was imprisoned for life.

_____ 11. She felt no malice toward the person who had been hired to replace her.

_____ 12. He had recently contracted a congenital malady.

_____ 13. A genial clerk took time to explain why my steam iron had malfunctioned.

_____ 14. The job he was given was not commensurate with his ability.

☐**EXERCISE 3** In your journal describe someone you know who is always complaining about ill health. Use some of these words: chronic, commiserate, malaise, dissuade, concur, malady.

MORPH—form

MORPH meaning *form* is an easy root to spot and will help clarify some difficult words. For example, **amorphous** [A without + MORPH form] refers to something that is without *form*, such as a speech that has not yet been organized, a poem that is still in an unformed state, a plan that has not yet taken shape, or some clay that is ready for the potter's wheel.

amorphous (uh mawr′ fus) [A without + MORPH form]—without definite form or shape. *His notes for his lecture were still in an amorphous state, without any plan or organization.*

ectomorphic (ek tuh mawr′ fik) [ECTO outside + MORPH form]—characterized by a slender physical build developed from the outside layer of the embryo. *With his ectomorphic build, he was never able to compete in football.*

endomorphic (en duh mawr′ fik) [ENDO inside + MORPH form]—characterized by prominence of the abdomen and other soft body parts developed from the inside layer of the embryo. *An endomorphic person has to struggle constantly against becoming overweight.*

mesomorphic (mez uh mawr′ fik) [MESO middle + MORPH form]—characterized by muscular or athletic build developed from the middle layer of the embryo. *The mesomorphic person tends to be successful in contact sports.*

metamorphosis (met uh mawr′ fuh sis) [META change + MORPH form]—change of form or shape. *A caterpillar undergoes a metamorphosis when it turns into a butterfly.*

Morpheus (mawr′ fē us)—in Greek mythology the god of dreams and of the forms that dreaming sleepers see. *Morpheus was so named because of the forms he controlled in people's dreams.*

morphine (mawr′ fēn)—a drug used to bring sleep or ease pain (named after Morpheus). *The doctor prescribed morphine for the agonizing pain.*

morphology (mawr fol′ uh jē) [MORPH form + -LOGY study of]—the branch of biology that makes a study of the form of animals or plants. *The professor specializes in the morphology of gophers.*

ALSO: anthropomorphic, anthropomorphism

□**EXERCISE 1**   Write the appropriate MORPH word.

1. She is the _____ type, muscular and good in sports.

2. He was studying _____, especially the forms of ferns.

3. _____ is a drug named after Morpheus, the god of dreams.

4. With her _____ build, she tends to put on weight.

5. An artist begins a sculpture with an _____ piece of clay.

6. My cousin is the _____ type, slender in build.

7. We observed the _____ of the tadpole into a frog.

☐**EXERCISE 2 REVIEW** Write C in front of each sentence in which all words are used correctly. Then in each remaining blank, write the word that should have been used.

_____ 1. She tried to efface from her mind the scene that had just taken place.

_____ 2. At the close of the service the minister pronounced the malediction.

_____ 3. Many cities saw the exodus of people from the inner city to the suburbs.

_____ 4. Taking away a tribe's way of getting food is really genocide.

_____ 5. The speaker was aware of the benevolent glances of his opponents.

_____ 6. She always tried to buy generic products because they are usually less expensive than brand name products.

_____ 7. We marveled at how the ancients had moved the monoliths at Stonehenge.

_____ 8. Eventually we will have to think in kilometers rather than in miles.

_____ 9. Her handling of the problem was so maladroit that everyone was annoyed.

☐**EXERCISE 3** REVIEW What name would you apply to a person

1. who studies or collects antiquities? _____

2. who studies the development and behavior of human beings? _____

3. who denies the existence of God? _____

4. who loves people and gives money to benefit them? _____

5. who disagrees with the government? _____

PAN—all

In his epic poem *Paradise Lost,* John Milton calls the capital of hell Pandemonium (PAN all + DAIMON demon), the home of *all* demons, a place of wild confusion and noise. Today **pandemonium** has come to mean any wild uproar or tumult.

panacea (pan uh sē' uh) [PAN all + AKOS remedy]—a remedy for all ills or difficulties. *People who join cults are often looking for a panacea for their troubles.*

Pan-American (pan uh mer' uh kun)—including all of America, both North and South. *He hopes to participate in the Pan-American games.*

panchromatic (pan krō mat' ik) [PAN all + CHROM color]—sensitive to light of all colors. *The panchromatic film gave him excellent pictures.*

pandemonium (pan duh mō' nē um) [PAN all + DAIMON demon]—the home of all demons in Milton's *Paradise Lost;* a wild uproar. *When the winning team returned, there was pandemonium.*

panoply (pan' uh plē) [PAN all + HOPLON armor]—a full suit of armor; ceremonial attire; any magnificent or impressive array. *The woods in their full panoply of autumn foliage were an invitation to photographers.*

panorama (pan uh ram' uh) [PAN all + HORAMA sight]—a view in all directions. *The panorama from the top of the Royal Gorge was awe-inspiring.*

pantheism (pan' thē iz um) [PAN all + THE god]—the doctrine that God is all the laws and forces of nature and the universe. *He turned from the formal religions to a belief in pantheism.* Also, the ancient belief in and worship of all gods. *Pantheism was the religion of early Rome.*

pantheon (pan' thē on) [PAN all + THE god]—a temple of all the gods. *They visited the Pantheon in Rome.* Also, the place of the idols of any group, or the idols themselves. *Eric Heiden skated his way into the pantheon of American Olympic heroes.*

pantomime (pan' tuh mīm) [PAN all + MIM to imitate]—a theatrical performance in which the actors play all the parts with gestures and without speaking. *Marcel Marceau has turned the ancient dramatic form of pantomime into an art.*

ALSO: pandemic, panegyric

☐**EXERCISE 1**   Write the appropriate PAN word.

1. If you invite 20 five-year-olds to a birthday party, you'd better be prepared for

   _____.

2. The patent medicine was supposed to be a _____ for all diseases.

3. His love of nature and reverence for natural laws almost amounted to

   _____.

4. It is worth climbing to the top of the cathedral to see the _____ of the city.

5. _____ by a good actor can be as expressive as dialogue.

6. The marching band was out on the football field in their full_____.

7. His goal was to make the _____ of famous tennis players.

8. They used _____ film for all their pictures of the Grand Canyon.

☐**EXERCISE 2   REVIEW**   Write C in front of each sentence in which all words are used correctly.

_____ 1. The statue was still only an amorphous chunk of clay in the sculptor's studio.

_____ 2. The conductor was looking for a monotone to complete the bass section of the choir.

_____ 3. When my car won't start, my only recourse is to call a taxi.

_____ 4. He had become interested in genealogy and was making lists of all his nineteenth-century progeny.

_____ 5. The circumspect approach of the diplomat proved effective in the delicate negotiations.

_____ 6. The mayor was a demagogue who worked unselfishly for the people in his district.

☐**EXERCISE 3**   Are you adding each day a word or two to your WORD LIST— words you hope to make a part of your permanent vocabulary?

PATH—feeling, suffering

Do you feel sympathy or empathy when the boy on stage has forgotten his speech? And do you feel apathy or antipathy toward the ideas a lecturer is presenting?

All four words—sympathy, empathy, apathy, and antipathy—describe *feelings* because they all contain the root PATH *feeling*. **Sympathy** [SYM together + PATH feeling) is literally *feeling* together with someone. **Empathy** [EM in + PATH feeling] is a stronger word, indicating that you identify with someone so closely that you *feel* "in" that person's position. **Apathy** [A without + PATH feeling] means lack of *feeling,* indifference. **Antipathy** [ANTI against + PATH feeling] means a *feeling* against someone or something, a strong dislike.

You will of course feel sympathy for the boy who is having stage fright, but if he happens to be your child, you will also feel empathy—identifying with him and participating in his suffering.

If the ideas a lecturer is presenting are boring, you'll feel apathy or indifference. You'll be apathetic, without feeling. But if you strongly disagree with the ideas, then you'll feel antipathy toward them and perhaps even toward the lecturer.

antipathy (an tip' uh thē) [ANTI against + PATH feeling]—a feeling against someone or something; a strong dislike. *His antipathy toward those who disagreed with him was obvious.*

apathetic (ap uh thet' ik) [A without + PATH feeling]—without feeling; indifferent. *When she failed to get a promotion, she became apathetic about her job and no longer did her best.*

apathy (ap' uh thē) [A without + PATH feeling]—a lack of feeling; indifference. *Voter apathy was to blame for the poor turnout on Election Day.*

empathy (em' puh thē) [EM in + PATH feeling]—*lit.* a feeling as if one were in the other person's place; an understanding so intimate that one participates in another's feelings. *Because he had been unemployed the year before, he now felt empathy for his unemployed friend.*

pathetic (puh thet' ik)—arousing feelings of pity. *Seeing the dog hunt for her missing pups was pathetic.*

pathological (path uh loj' i kul)—caused by disease. *It was finally determined that her inability to concentrate was pathological.*

pathology (pa thol' uh jē) [PATH suffering + -LOGY study of]—*lit.* the study of suffering; the scientific study of the nature of disease, especially the structural and functional changes caused by disease. *The doctor preferred doing laboratory research in pathology rather than treating patients.*

pathos (pā' thos)—a quality, especially in literature, that arouses feelings of pity. *My sister loves movies full of pathos, movies she can cry over.*

psychopathic (sī kō path′ ik) [PSYCH mind + PATH suffering]—*lit.* suffering in the mind; mentally disordered. *The search for the psychopathic killer ended in his capture.*

sympathy (sim′ puh thē) [SYM together + PATH feeling]—*lit.* a feeling together with someone or something; a feeling for another person. *Everyone felt sympathy for the girl who lost the race.*

ALSO: pathogenic, telepathy

□**EXERCISE 1** Write the appropriate PATH word.

1. His yawn indicated that he was _____.

2. She feels such _____ for her son in his struggle to make the team that it's almost as if she were trying to make it herself.

3. The defendant was diagnosed as _____ by the court psychiatrist and was sent to a mental hospital.

4. My father has an _____ toward artificial flowers.

5. Her abnormal distrust of everyone was obviously _____.

6. The _____ in that movie led to a lot of sniffles.

7. He's lost interest in politics and has become so _____ that he doesn't even vote.

□**EXERCISE 2 REVIEW** Match each word with its definition.

A. biennial	C. anthropoid	E. amorphous
B. chronic	D. benevolent	F. anthropologist

_____ 1. inclined to do good

_____ 2. without definite form or shape

_____ 3. occurring every two years

_____ 4. resembling human beings

_____ 5. one who studies the development and behavior of human beings

_____ 6. continuing for a long time

PED—foot

Two words containing PED were originally concerned with getting one's foot in an entanglement. **Impede** [IM in + PED foot] meant to get one's *foot* into an entanglement and thus hinder one's progress. Through the years it has lost the meaning of the foot in an entanglement and now has come to mean merely to hinder the progress of. **Expedite** [EX out + PED foot] originally meant to get one's *foot* out of an entanglement and thus to speed up one's progress. Expedite too has lost the meaning of the foot in an entanglement and today means merely to speed the progress of, to help along. You might say that a poor vocabulary will impede your progress in college whereas a large vocabulary will expedite your progress by helping you read with more understanding.

centipede (sen' tuh pēd) [CENT hundred + PED foot]—a wormlike invertebrate popularly supposed to have a hundred feet. *In the tropics, centipedes invaded our cottage.*

expedient (ek spē' dē unt) [EX out + PED foot]—*lit.* foot out of an entanglement; advantageous; useful in getting a desired result. *It might be expedient to start writing your paper long before it is due.*

expedite (ek' spuh dīt) [EX out + PED foot]—*lit.* to get the foot out of an entanglement; to speed the progress of; to help along. *To expedite your registration, fill out the forms ahead of time.*

expedition (ek spuh dish' un) [EX out + PED foot]—*lit.* freeing the foot; a journey for a definite purpose. *The expedition to the North Pole brought back much scientific information.*

impede (im pēd') [IM in + PED foot]—*lit.* to get the foot in an entanglement; to hinder the progress of. *An inability to read rapidly may impede one's academic progress.*

impediment (im ped' uh munt) [IM in + PED foot]—*lit.* entanglement of the foot; anything that hinders. *The famous Greek orator Demosthenes had to overcome a speech impediment.*

pedal (ped' ul) [PED foot]—a lever operated by the foot. *The little fellow could not reach the pedals on his bike.*

pedestrian (pu des' trē un) [PED foot]—one who goes on foot; also, commonplace or dull, as a pedestrian style of writing. *This is a dangerous corner for pedestrians.*

pedigree (ped' uh grē) [from the French PIED foot + DE of + GRUE crane]—*lit.* the foot of a crane, so called because the three-line diagram used to indicate descent looks like a crane's foot; a record of ancestry. *The collie's pedigree made him a valuable show dog.*

quadruped (kwahd' roo ped) [QUADR four + PED foot]—a four-footed animal. *Most mammals are quadrupeds.*

ALSO: biped, pedestal, pedicure, pedometer

☐**EXERCISE 1**   Write the appropriated PED word.

1. Reading my reference materials ahead of time will _____ my progress in writing my paper.

2. She thought it might be _____ to invite the boss to dinner.

3. Spraining his ankle early in the season is going to _____ his progress toward the championship.
4. She couldn't imaging anyone wanting a dog without a _____.

5. His unpopular voting record is an _____ in his reelection campaign.

☐**EXERCISE 2   REVIEW**   Underline the appropriate word.

1. I'm tired of cold winters and am looking for an (equable, equitable) climate.
2. She had an (ingenuous, ingenious) way of avoiding her after-school chores.
3. The backers of the bill were (ebullient, disconsolate) when it passed.
4. He and his wife weren't troubled by the (diversion, disparity) in their salaries.
5. The perimeter of a property is the distance (across, around) it.
6. Her poetry was (euphonious, equivocal) and pleasant to listen to.

☐**EXERCISE 3   REVIEW**   Can you read this paragraph with no hesitancy about the meaning of all the words? If you are not sure of any word, look it up in the Word Index.

The results of the 1990 census have given us a demographic picture of the United States. Census forms were mailed to each dwelling to expedite the task of counting the entire population. Advertising was used to overcome the apathy that might have kept people from filling out the forms. The facts gathered were especially important to cities and states with population increases, for they are now the beneficiaries of increased funding from government programs.

☐**EXERCISE 4**   In your journal list two things that have impeded your progress in mastering the words in this book and two things that have expedited your progress.

PHIL—to love

A word containing PHIL will have something to do with *love*. Philosophy [PHIL to love + SOPH wise] is the *love* of wisdom. A **bibliophile** [BIBL book + PHIL to love] is one who *loves* books. And a **philanthropist** [PHIL to love + ANTHROP human] is one who *loves* human beings, particularly one who gives money to benefit humanity (see p. 20).

Anglophile (ang′ gluh fīl) [ANGL English + PHIL to love]—one who greatly admires England, its customs, and its people. *A confirmed Anglophile, she spends every summer in England.*

bibliophile (bib′ lē uh fīl) [BIBL book + PHIL to love]—one who loves books; a book collector. *We discovered a small bookstore owned by a true bibliophile.*

philatelist (fi lat′ uh list) [PHIL to love + ATELEIA tax exemption (the stamp showed that the postage had been prepaid, and the receiver was exempt from further charge)]—one who loves stamps; a stamp collector. *As a philatelist, she was interested in collecting foreign stamps.*

philharmonic (fil hahr mon′ ik) [PHIL to love + HARMONIA harmony]—*lit.* loving harmony; devoted to music; a symphony orchestra. *That winter we heard the New York Philharmonic Orchestra.*

philodendron (fil uh den′ drun) [PHIL to love + DENDR tree]—*lit.* loving trees; a tropical climbing plant that likes the shade of trees. *She cultivated the philodendron plant for its showy heart-shaped leaves.*

philosopher (fi los′ uh fur) [PHIL to love + SOPH wise]—one who loves and pursues wisdom through reasoning. *Immanuel Kant was one of the great philosophers of the eighteenth century.*

philosophy (fi los′ uh fē) [PHIL to love + SOPH wise]—the love and pursuit of wisdom through reasoning. *Socrates valued philosophy more than anything else.*

ALSO: Philadelphia, philanthropist, philanthropy, Philip, philippic, philology

☐**EXERCISE 1**   Match each word with its definition.

A. philharmonic
B. bibliophile

C. philatelist
D. philosopher

E. Anglophile
F. philanthropist

_____ 1. one who loves books

_____ 2. one who admires England

_____ 3. one who loves human beings and gives money to benefit humanity

_____ 4. a stamp collector

_____ 5. one who loves and pursues wisdom through reasoning

_____ 6. loving harmony, devoted to music, a symphony orchestra

☐**EXERCISE 2   REVIEW**   Underline the appropriate word.

1. The study of the forms of animals and plants is called (morphology, pathology).
2. Through her study of (entomology, etymology) she has learned the derivation of many words and thus improved her vocabulary.
3. The company was (monolithic, amorphous), with a strong central office controlling many branches.
4. He took a course in (calligraphy, topography) to improve his penmanship.
5. The cashier was accused of (malapropism, malfeasance) when the deficit was discovered.
6. She felt (perfidy, antipathy) toward the course, hating every moment of it.
7. The actor used (pantomime, pantheism) rather than words to present the character.
8. An interest in word roots will (impede, expedite) your learning new words.
9. The supervisor found the employee guilty of one lie after another and branded him (maladroit, perfidious).
10. Saying that entering a new college is like jumping into an icy lake is an (analogy, anecdote).
11. The (philanthropist, philatelist) showed us his collection of stamps.
12. His name was added to the (panoply, pantheon) of famous runners.
13. The census has brought about a more (equable, equitable) distribution of government funds.
14. He took the picture with a (panchromatic, philharmonic) film.

☐**EXERCISE 3**   In your journal describe your best friend, looking back through this book to find the most effective words to describe that person.

PHOB—fear

Do you refuse to stand on the observation platform of a tall building? If so, perhaps you have **acrophobia,** an excessive *fear* of high places. Do you avoid elevators? If so, you may be suffering from **claustrophobia,** an excessive *fear* of closed places.

acrophobia (ak ruh fō′ bē uh) [ACRO high + PHOB fear]—an excessive or illogical fear of high places. *Because of her acrophobia, she refused to approach the rim of the canyon.*

claustrophobia (klos truh fō′ bē uh) [CLAUS to close + PHOB fear]—an excessive or illogical fear of enclosed places. *His claustrophobia made him prefer an office that opened onto a balcony.*

hydrophobia (hi druh fō′ bē uh) [HYDR water + PHOB fear]—an abnormal fear of water. Also, rabies (rabies was first called hydrophobia because victims were unable to swallow water). *There was an outbreak of hydrophobia among the dogs of the area.*

phobia (fō′ bē uh)—an excessive or illogical fear of some particular thing or situation. *Her fear of dogs has really become a phobia.*

phobic (fō′ bik)—excessively fearful. *She had a phobic desire to avoid large crowds.*

photophobia (fo tuh fō′ bē uh) [PHOT light + PHOB fear]—an abnormal intolerance of light. *Because of photophobia, he had to wear tinted glasses.*

technophobia (tek nuh fō′ bē uh) [TECHN skill + PHOB fear]—*lit.* a fear of technology; computer anxiety. *She finally overcame her technophobia and completed a course called "Introduction to BASIC."*

xenophobia (zen uh fō′ bē uh) [XENO foreigner + PHOB fear]—fear or hatred of foreigners or strangers. *Extreme patriotism may turn into xenophobia.*

☐**EXERCISE 1** Write the appropriate PHOB word.

1. His eye problems were diagnosed as _____.

2. Because of his _____ dread of failing, he was constantly uneasy.

3. Their lack of understanding of foreigners amounted to _____.

4. She claimed she got _____ from working in a small room with no windows.

5. Wild rabbits can sometimes be the carriers of _____.

6. Going out on the high balcony bothered him because he suffered from _____.

7. A severe attack of _____ made her decide to keep her old manual typewriter.

8. His dislike of public speaking has almost become a _____.

☐**EXERCISE 2 REVIEW** Give the meaning of each root and a word in which it is found.

	MEANING	WORD
1. DICT	_____	_____
2. DIS, DI, DIF	_____	_____
3. EQU	_____	_____
4. EU	_____	_____
5. EX, ES, E	_____	_____
6. FID	_____	_____
7. GEN	_____	_____
8. GRAPH, GRAM	_____	_____
9. LOG	_____	_____
10. -LOGY	_____	_____
11. LOQU, LOC	_____	_____
12. MAL	_____	_____
13. METER, METR	_____	_____
14. MIT, MIS, MISS	_____	_____
15. MONO	_____	_____
16. MORPH	_____	_____
17. PAN	_____	_____
18. PATH	_____	_____
19. PED	_____	_____
20. PHIL	_____	_____
21. PHOB	_____	_____

PHON—sound

Any word containing PHON always has something to do with *sound*. A **symphony** [SYM together + PHON sound] is literally *sounds* together, presumably pleasant sounds. If a *sound* is harsh or unpleasant, it is called **cacophony** [CACO bad + PHON sound] whereas smooth and harmonious *sounds*, especially words or phrases that please the ear, are called **euphony** [EU good + PHON sound] (see p. 54).

cacophony (ka kof' uh nē) [CACO bad + PHON sound]—*lit.* bad sounds; disagreeable or discordant sounds. *Only a mother can enjoy the cacophony of her child's violin practice.*

megaphone (meg' uh fōn) [MEGA large + PHON sound]—*lit.* large sound; a cone-shaped device for making the sound of the voice greater. *The cheerleaders all had megaphones.*

microphone (mī' kruh fōn) [MICRO small + PHON sound]—an instrument for intensifying weak (small) sounds. *The speaker could not be heard clearly because he did not speak into the microphone.*

phonetics (fuh net' iks)—the branch of language study dealing with speech sounds and their symbols. *A knowledge of phonetic symbols is an aid in learning to speak a new language.*

phonics (fon' iks)—the use of the sounds of letters and groups of letters in teaching beginners to read. *The teacher used the phonics method for teaching the children to read.*

phonograph (fō' nuh graf) [PHON sound + GRAPH to write]—a machine for playing recorded (written on a disk) sounds. *My grandmother has an antique phonograph.*

polyphonic (pol ē fon' ik) [POLY many + PHON sound]—having two or more independent melodies all harmonizing. *A polyphonic composition has two or more melodies combined.*

saxophone (sak' suh fōn) [SAX (after Adolphe Sax, the inventor) + PHON sound]—a wind instrument. *My brother now plays a saxophone.*

stereophonic (ster ē ō fon' ik) [STEREO solid + PHON sound]—*lit.* solid sound; giving a multidimensional effect to sound. *A stereophonic record sounds like live music because it contains two separate sound tracks.*

symphony (sim' fuh nē) [SYM together + PHON sound]—*lit.* sounds together; an orchestra; music written for an orchestra. *Our local symphony orchestra will give a concert in May.*

ALSO: antiphonal, euphonious, euphony, telephone

☐**EXERCISE 1** Write the appropriate PHON word.

1. It was good to get out of the _____ of the office with its phones ringing and people chattering.

2. The several melodies are combined into an unusual _____ composition.

3. The _____ was named after its inventor, Adolphe Sax.

4. Even if I used a _____, I doubt if anyone would hear what I'm trying to say in all this din.

5. His knowledge of _____ helped him pronounce French words correctly.

☐**EXERCISE 2 REVIEW** Write C in front of each sentence in which all words are used correctly. Then in each remaining blank, write the word that should have been used.

_____ 1. At the auction I bought a bona fide Singer sewing machine.

_____ 2. Her college course in ornithology led to her lifelong hobby of bird watching.

_____ 3. I won't let anything impede my progress in learning new words.

_____ 4. Anyone with acrophobia will not want to go into the cave.

_____ 5. An emissary brought greetings from his country.

_____ 6. It is not only philatelists who like the new commemorative stamps.

_____ 7. Only a bibliophile would be interested in that tattered old book.

_____ 8. The two countries agreed that each would quit dropping missives on the other country.

_____ 9. Her inability to sit still for even a few moments was diagnosed as pathological.

_____ 10. To expurgate is to remove offensive language from written material.

_____ 11. The secretary felt circumscribed by all the regulations she had to follow.

☐**EXERCISE 3** In your journal list the best examples of cacophony that you can think of.

POST—after

Preposterous is made up of PRE *before* and POST *after* and originally meant having the before part where the after part should be, as a horse with its head where its tail should be. Such a *before-after* animal would be preposterous or absurd. And so today anything contrary to nature, reason, or common sense is called preposterous.

postdate (pōs dāt′) [POST after + DATE date]—to date a check or other document with a future date rather than the actual date. *Because I had no money in the bank, I postdated my check.*

posterior (po stir′ ē ur)—located behind (as opposed to anterior, located in front). *The posterior legs of the jackrabbit are stronger than the anterior ones.*

posterity (po ster′ uh tē)—those who come after; future generations. *Posterity will determine the value of his writing.*

postgraduate (pōst graj′ uh wut)—relating to a course of study after college graduation. *I look forward to taking a couple of postgraduate courses.*

posthumously (pos′ choo mus li)—after the death of the father, as a child born posthumously; after the death of the author, as a book published posthumously; after one's death, as an award received posthumously. *The medal of honor was awarded to him posthumously.*

Postimpressionist (pōst im presh′ uh nist)—*lit.* after the Impressionists; a school of painting in France in the late nineteenth century that followed the Impressionists. *Cézanne and Matisse were Postimpressionists.*

postlude (pōst′ lood) [POST after + LUD to play]—a piece of music played after a church service. *The organist played a Bach fugue as a postlude.*

post meridiem (pōst muh rid′ ē um) [POST after + MERIDI noon]—(abbreviated P.M.) after noon. *The committee will meet at 3 P.M.*

postmortem (post mor′ tum) [POST after + MORT death]—an examination after death; an autopsy. *The postmortem revealed the cause of his death.*

postpone (pōs pōn′) [POST after + PON to put]—to put off until afterward. *I usually postpone studying until the last minute.*

postscript (pō′ skript) [POST after + SCRIPT to write]—a note written after the main body of a letter (abbreviated P.S.). *Often the most interesting part of her letter was the postscript.*

preposterous (pri pos′ tur us) [PRE before + POST after]—*lit.* having the before part where the after part should be; contrary to nature, reason, or common sense; absurd. *The idea of flying to the moon was once considered preposterous.*

ALSO: postnatal, postnuptial, postoperative

☐**EXERCISE 1**   Write the appropriate POST word.

1. Now that the poet is dead, some of his poems are being published

   _____.

2. They prepared a time capsule for _____.

3. Traveling faster than sound was once considered a _____ idea.

4. The _____ of a giraffe's body is less developed than the anterior.

5. During the organ _____ the congregation left the church.

6. An entire gallery in the art museum was devoted to the works of the

   _____.

7. Because the death was unexpected, a _____ was required.

☐**EXERCISE 2**   **REVIEW**   Underline the appropriate word.

1. With no thought of (emolument, equity), the teacher spent hours helping the immigrants.

2. He would (eulogize, excoriate) his wife for the slightest error in her cooking.

3. They talked about subjects as (disparate, equivalent) as mud pies and ballet.

4. The applicant tended to (equivocate, expurgate) when his former job was mentioned.

5. I was (dismantled, disconcerted) when they excluded me from their plans.

6. A distrust of foreigners is called (technophobia, xenophobia).

7. The government was constantly threatened by the (dissidents, automatons).

8. A devoted Anglophile, he even uses a (monocle, trident) instead of glasses.

9. The manager of the hotel tried to create an (ambivalence, ambience) of luxury.

10. The society planned (biannual, biennial) meetings so the members could see each other at least twice a year.

11. The organist played a (prologue, postlude) at the end of the service.

12. He checked his distance traveled by the (barometer, odometer).

13. The surgeon was doing research in (pathology, phonetics).

☐**EXERCISE 3**   In your journal write about a trip you enjoyed, using at least two words that are new in your vocabulary.

PRE—before

PRE at the beginning of a word always means *before* and is easy to understand in such words as **preschool, premature, prehistoric, premeditate, prejudge,** and **precaution.** But sometimes the meaning is not so obvious. For example, **precocious** [PRE before + COQUERE to cook, to ripen] originally applied to fruit that ripened early (before time). Today it describes someone who has matured earlier than usual, particularly mentally. Children who are unusually smart for their years are called precocious. They have ripened early!

preamble (prē′ am bul) [PRE before + AMBUL to walk]—*lit.* a walking before; a preliminary statement to a document. *Have you read the Preamble to the Constitution?*

precedent (pres′ uh dunt) [PRE before + CED to go]—an act that goes before and may serve as an example for later acts. *His giving his prize to charity set a precedent that later winners followed.*

precipitate (pri sip′ uh tāt) [PRE before + CAPIT head]—*lit.* to dash head-first; to hasten the occurrence of. *The scandal precipitated his ruin.*

precise (pri sīs′) [PRE before + CIS to cut]—*lit.* to cut off unnecessary parts beforehand; sharply defined and exact. *Her descriptions were always precise.*

preclude (pri klōōd′) [PRE before + CLUD to shut]—*lit.* to shut out beforehand; to make impossible by a previous action; to prevent. *His poor record with that company may preclude his getting another job.*

precocious (pri kō′ shus) [PRE before + COQUERE to cook, ripen]—*lit.* ripened before time; prematurely developed, as a precocious child. *The child was precocious, having learned to read at four.*

predilection (pred l ek′ shun) [PRE before + DILIGERE to love]—*lit.* to love before others; a preference. *Her predilection for classical music kept her from being an impartial judge in the music contest.*

preeminent (prē em′ uh nunt) [PRE before + EMINERE to stand out]—standing out before all others. *Edison was preeminent among the scientists of his day.*

prejudice (prej′ ud us) [PRE before + JUD judge]—a judgment formed beforehand without examination of the facts. *She finally realized that her intolerance of the newcomers was simply unfounded prejudice.*

prelude (prel′ ōōd) [PRE before + LUD to play]—an introductory piece of music; a concert piece for piano or orchestra. *She played a Chopin prelude at the recital.* Also, an introductory performance or action preceding a more important one. *The passage of that law was the prelude to further civil rights legislation.*

preponderant (pri pon′ dur unt) [PRE before + PONDER weight]—outweighing; having more power or importance. *The preponderant theme of the speakers was the future welfare of the institution.*

prerequisite (prē rek′ wuh zit)—something required beforehand. *Algebra is a prerequisite for geometry.*

presage (pres′ ij) [PRE before + SAGIRE to perceive]—to perceive beforehand; to predict. *Lack of cooperation among the employees presages trouble in the industry. Those dark clouds presage a storm.*

prevail (pri vāl′) [PRE before + VAL to be strong]—to be strong before all others; to win, as to prevail over the other contestants. *After years of practice, he finally prevailed over his challengers.*

prevent (pri vent′) [PRE before + VEN to come]—*lit.* to come before in order to keep from happening; to hinder. *Good farming techniques can prevent erosion.*

unprecedented (un pres′ uh den tid) [UN not + PRE before + CED to go]—never having happened before. *The sales manager took an unprecedented step when he gave the job to a teenager.*

ALSO: precede, precursor, predestination, predict, predominant, preempt, premise, preposterous, prerogative, prescribe, presentiment, preside, president, pretentious, previous

---

☐**EXERCISE 1** Write the appropriate PRE word.

1. The bank failure was _____ by the sudden fall in interest rates.
2. She insisted that her child was _____ rather than average.
3. The court decision set a _____ that was followed for many years.
4. I have a _____ for blue and find it hard to buy any other color.
5. His strong stand against forced retirement was _____ in that company. No one had ever taken such a stand before.

6. After publishing her research, she was considered _____ in her field.
7. The testimony of the medical doctor was _____ in the minds of the jury.
8. The early morning clouds _____ a stormy day.

9. His unwillingness to negotiate _____ any hope of a reconciliation with his boss.
10. The ability to use a computer is a _____ for the job.

PRO—forward, before, for, forth

Do you tend to put off unpleasant tasks until a future time? If so, you probably have a **propensity** [PRO forward + PENS to hang] (a hanging *forward* or inclination) to **procrastinate** [PRO forward + CRAS tomorrow] (to push tasks *forward* until tomorrow). When it comes to studying, many students have a propensity to procrastinate.

proceed (prō sēd') [PRO forward + CEED to go]—to go forward. *Now that the members are all here, the meeting will proceed.*

proclaim (prō klām') [PRO forth + CLAM to cry out]—to announce officially and publicly. *The day was proclaimed a holiday.*

proclivity (prō kliv' uh tē) [PRO forward + CLIVUS slope]—*lit.* a slope forward; an inclination toward something, especially toward something objectionable. *Her proclivity to exaggerate finally led to her losing her job.*

procrastinate (prō kras' tuh nāt) [PRO forward + CRAS tomorrow]—*lit.* to push forward until tomorrow; to put off doing something until a future time. *I always procrastinate about cleaning the house.*

profuse (pruh fyōōs') [PRO forth + FUS to pour]—pouring forth freely; generous. *The mechanic was profuse in her apologies.*

profusion (pruh fyōō' zhun) [PRO forth + FUS to pour]—*lit.* a pouring forth; an abundance. *The profusion of wildflowers on the hill delighted us.*

projectile (pruh jek' tul) [PRO forward + JECT to throw]—something thrown forward by force; a missile. *The projectile just missed a populated area.*

promontory (prom' un tōr ē) [PRO forward + MONT mountain]—a high peak of land or rock (mountain) jutting forward into the sea. *From the promontory we had a view of the entire area.*

promotion (pruh mō' shun) [PRO forward + MOT to move]—a moving forward, as to a better job. *My sister is hoping for a promotion.*

propel (pruh pel') [PRO forward + PEL to push]—to push or drive forward. *Against his wishes he was propelled into the race.*

propensity (pruh pen' suh tē) [PRO forward + PENS to hang]—*lit.* a hanging forward: a natural inclination. *He has a propensity for putting things off.*

(Propensity and proclivity are close synonyms.)

proponent (pruh pō' nunt) [PRO before + PON to put]—*lit.* one who puts something before people; one who argues in favor of something; an advocate. *A leading proponent of recycling is speaking tonight.*

prospectus (pruh spek' tus) [PRO forward + SPECT to look]—*lit.* a looking forward; a printed description of a proposed enterprise. *The prospectus made the new subdivision look inviting.*

protuberant (prō too′ bur unt) [PRO forth + TUBER swelling]—bulging. *From childhood he had been conscious of his protuberant nose.*

provide (pruh vīd′) [PRO before + VID to see]—*lit.* to see beforehand; to get ready beforehand. *The college will provide transportation for the team.*

provident (prov′ uh dunt) [PRO before + VID to see]—*lit.* seeing beforehand; making provision for the future. *If he had been more provident, he wouldn't be in need now.*

provision (pruh vizh′ un) [PRO before + VIS to see]—a seeing beforehand; a preparation for the future. *The parents had made provision for their son's college expenses.*

ALSO: improvise, proclamation, produce, progenitor, progeny, prognosis, prognosticate, program, prologue, promulgate, pronoun, prophet, propitiate, propitious, proscribe, protracted, provocation

---

☐**EXERCISE 1** Write the appropriate PRO word.

1. The _____ for the investment fund was tempting.

2. His _____ or _____ for wasting time may cost him his job.

3. She's a _____ of the amendment to ban disposable bottles.

4. All his children inherited his _____ ears.

5. Whenever I _____, someone always quotes the old epigram, "Don't put off until tomorrow. . . ."

6. His tardiness was always followed by a _____ of excuses.

7. We stood on the _____ and looked out over the ocean.

8. Always a _____ person, he had taken care of his family's needs before he left for the month.

9. With _____ thanks, she accepted the award.

RE—back, again

What would you do with a recalcitrant child? First you might have to figure out the meaning of **recalcitrant**. Since RE means *back* and CALC means *heel*, recalcitrant means literally kicking *back* the heels. Once used in referring to horses and mules, it now is applied to human beings. Therefore a recalcitrant child would be one who is kicking *back*, obstinate, stubbornly rebellious.

The meaning of many words that begin with RE are simple: **return** is simply to turn *again;* **recall** is to call *again,* and **reconstruct** is to construct *again.* Here are some more familiar words that you won't need pronunciation helps or sentence examples for.

recede [RE back + CED to go]—to go back, as a river recedes from its banks

receive [RE again + CAP to take]—*lit.* to take again; to take something offered

recreation [RE again + CREAT to create]—*lit.* a creating again; the refreshment of mind or body through some form of play or amusement

referee [RE back + FER to carry]—one to whom questions are carried back; an official in a sports contest

remit [RE back + MIT to send]—to send back, as to remit payment

reside [RE back + SID to sit]—*lit.* to sit back; to dwell, as to reside in a house

residue [RE back + SID to sit]—*lit.* that which sits back; the part that remains after part has been separated away, as the residue in the bottom of a vase

retain [RE back + TEN to hold]—to hold back or keep in one's possession

revenue [RE back + VEN to come]—money that comes back from an investment or other source; taxes and other income collected by a government

revise [RE again + VIS to see]—to see again in order to correct errors

revive [RE again + VIV to live]—to cause to live again

And here are some less familiar words.

recalcitrant (ri kal′ suh trunt) [RE back + CALC heel]—*lit.* kicking back the heels; obstinate; stubbornly rebellious. *It's useless to argue with her when she's in a recalcitrant mood.*

recant (ri kant′) [RE back + CANT to sing]—to renounce a belief formerly held, especially in a formal or public manner. *The judge chose to recant publicly his former stand on capital punishment.*

recession (ri sesh′ un) [RE back + CESS to go]—a period of reduced economic activity. *The government feared a business recession.*

recluse (rek' lōōs) [RE back + CLUS to shut]—one who lives shut back from the world. *The poet Emily Dickinson lived as a recluse in her house in Amherst.*

remiss (ri mis') [RE back + MISS to send]—*lit.* sent back; negligent; lax in attending to duty. *I've been remiss about doing my exercises.*

remission (ri mish' un) [RE back + MISS to send]—*lit.* a sending back; a lessening, as a remission of disease; forgiveness, as remission of sins. *He enjoyed periods of remission from his illness.*

Renaissance (ren' uh sahns) [RE again + NASC to be born]—a rebirth; the revival of classical art, literature, and learning in Europe in the four-teenth, fifteenth, and sixteenth centuries. *Michelangelo was an artist of the Renaissance.*

resilience (ri zil' yunts) [RE again + SIL to leap]—*lit.* to leap again; the ability to recover quickly from illness, change, or misfortune. *With her customary resilience, she bounced back after her long illness.*

revert (ri vurt') [RE back + VERT to turn]—*lit.* to turn back; to return to a former habit or condition. *Occasionally she would revert to her child-hood dialect.*

ALSO: irrevocable, rebel, recapitulate, reclaim, recourse, recur, recurrent, reflect, refractory, reject, repel, respect, retort, revoke, revolve

---

☐EXERCISE 1   Write the appropriate RE word.

1. They were afraid to make any investments for fear there would be a

   _____.

2. He had never been an unruly or _____ child.

3. Occasionaly, however, he would _____ to infant behavior.

4. One needs plenty of _____ to cope with all the disappointments in that job.

5. She had a few weeks of good health during a _____ of her illness.

6. Living like a _____, he avoids all social contacts.

7. Realizing that she had been _____ about answering letters, she spent the evening at the typewriter.

8. The candidate has taken such a strong stand that for him to _____ would be unthinkable.

☐**EXERCISE 2 REVIEW** Write C in front of each sentence in which all words are used correctly. Then in each remaining blank, write the word that should have been used.

_____ 1. Deciding to emigrate from their homeland, they moved to Canada.

_____ 2. Federal laws are attempting to eradicate sexual discrimination.

_____ 3. They watched the smokestack emit pollutants.

_____ 4. She embroidered her monograph on all her towels.

_____ 5. The public was becoming aware of the demagoguery in the mayor's speeches.

_____ 6. You can count on his resilience to help him make a comeback even when he loses.

_____ 7. We were amazed at the profusion of flowers in their garden.

_____ 8. She decided to take a course in astrology at the university.

☐**EXERCISE 3 REVIEW** Here is a paragraph with eight words you have studied. If you are not sure of the meaning of any of them, list those words below and check in the Word Index to locate the pages where they are explained. Finally read the paragraph aloud. Perhaps after you have finished this exercise, a few of these words will find their way into your conversation.

I've read that a large vocabulary *presages* success both in college and in one's career. The idea sounds *credible,* and I'm now taking more interest in *etymology.* I've become a real word *addict* and am no longer *diffident* about using new words. Sometimes my friends are *discomfited* by my new hobby, but gradually even they are discovering the *ebullient* feeling that comes from using *precise* words.

☐**EXERCISE 4 REVIEW** Here, taken from magazine articles, are some sentences containing words you have studied. Are you sure of the meaning of every word? For any words you don't remember, consult the Word Index.

1. Natchez boasts it is the oldest city on the Mississippi River and has the largest collection of antebellum homes and buildings in the South.

2. The prime minister excoriated the new Labor Party leaders.

3. Concerning his first experience of weightlessness, the astronaut said, "I was in an almost euphoric condition."

4. The shah's pursuit of his own goals had engendered opposition from the intelligentsia.

5. Shirley MacLaine highlights the dances' meaning with a panoply of facial expressions.

6. The deadly plague reached across the Mediterranean from Africa during the first pandemic, beginning in A.D. 541.

7. The basis of Deng Xiao-ping's philosophy is summed up in his oft-quoted dictum "It doesn't matter whether a cat is black or white so long as it catches mice."

8. The human propensity to test the worthiness of a thing by seeing how well it stands up to abuse—the instinct to kick the tires of a used car—is an ancient habit.

9. The success of the government's economic programs has also given rise to unprecedented problems.

10. The result has been a flood of novel investment and savings devices. Moreover, there has grown up a cacophony of conflicting claims that is bewildering investors.

11. Two hundred researchers from nine countries meeting in Snowmass, Colorado, reached a consensus: CFCs *are* causing the ozone gap.

☐**EXERCISE 5** As a review of some of the roots you have learned, try to make a root chain similar to the one on page 2. Start with a word like *autobiography* or *geology,* and refer to the preceding pages to find the words you need. You may have to make several starts before you get a chain of the length you want. When you are satisfied, copy your chain on one of the blank pages at the end of this book.

SCRIB, SCRIPT—to write

In Europe in the fifth century a monk copied a manuscript, thus becoming the first European **scribe**. Before long, entire monasteries were founded to copy scriptural and literary texts. The scribes copied the texts laboriously in black, glossy letters; then other monks illuminated the capital letters with red pigment and gold leaf. Sometimes the making of a single book would occupy many years or even the lifetime of a monk.

ascribe (uh skrīb′) [AD to + SCRIB to write]—*lit.* to write to; to attribute. *His parents ascribed his actions to his eagerness to succeed.*

conscription (kun skrip′ shun) [CON together + SCRIPT to write]—*lit.* names written together; an enforced enrollment or military draft. *Conscription was often necessary to provide a large army.*

inscribe (in skrīb′) [IN in + SCRIB to write]—originally, to engrave words in stone; now, to write in, as the dedication of a book. *The author inscribed my copy of her book.*

manuscript (man′ yuh skript) [MANU hand + SCRIPT to write]—originally, something written by hand; now, a composition for publication. *He sent his manuscript to the publisher.*

nondescript (non′ di skript) [NON not + SCRIPT to write]—not easy to write about or describe, lacking in distinctive qualities. *Even though her outfit was nondescript, she was still the most striking person in the room.*

prescribe (pri skrīb′) [PRE before + SCRIB to write]—to write down a rule beforehand; in medicine, to order a treatment. *The doctor prescribed an antibiotic.*

proscribe (prō skrīb′) [PRO before + SCRIB to write]—in ancient Rome, to publish the name of one condemned to death; now, to condemn or forbid as harmful. *Some religions proscribe abortion.*

scribe (skrīb)—one who copies manuscripts. *In ancient Israel the scribes copied the Scriptures.*

script (skript)—handwriting; also, the written copy of a play used by actors to learn their lines. *She was studying the script for her part in the play.*

Scripture (skrip′ chur)—originally, anything written; now, the Bible. *The library owns an early edition of the Scripture.*

subscribe (sub skrīb′) [SUB under + SCRIB to write]—to write one's name on an agreement, as to subscribe to a magazine; also, to support or give approval to an idea. *Congress subscribed to the foreign policy of the president.*

transcribe (tran skrīb′) [TRANS over + SCRIB to write]—to write over again, as to transcribe notes. *After taking dictation in shorthand, he immediately transcribed his notes on the word processor.*

ALSO: circumscribe, describe, postscript, scribble, subscription, transcript

☐**EXERCISE 1**   Write the appropriate SCRIB, SCRIPT word.

1. They will probably _____ the failure of their plan to lack of funds.
2. His clothes were always _____ and unpressed.
3. It's wise to _____ one's class notes immediately after taking them.
4. During times of peace _____ is unnecessary.
5. Do you _____ to all his new ideas?
6. The court has _____ racial discrimination in housing.

☐**EXERCISE 2   REVIEW**   Write C in front of each sentence in which all words are used correctly.

_____ 1. The ancient Roman belief in many gods is called pantheism.

_____ 2. The proponents of the metric system are trying to bring the United States into line with the rest of the world.

_____ 3. To procrastinate about doing an unpleasant task is simply to postpone it.

_____ 4. The prospectus for the new housing development made us want to move there.

_____ 5. Because her parents had not been provident, she was never in want.

_____ 6. The Renaissance in Italy was a revolt of the common people.

_____ 7. The captain had set a precedent of fair play that his teammates now followed.

_____ 8. The Impressionists came before the Postimpressionists.

_____ 9. No one has ever doubted the credibility of our governor.

_____ 10. Her excellent vocabulary was an impediment to her reading.

_____ 11. The child's fear of the dark has become a phobia.

_____ 12. Because she was ambidextrous, she had to travel in a wheelchair.

_____ 13. They celebrated their centennial wedding anniversary when they had been married fifty years.

_____ 14. Television was the precursor of radio.

_____ 15. It was pleasant to watch the play in the outdoor amphitheater.

_____ 16. From the top floor of the building we could see the panorama of the entire countryside.

_____ 17. The batter was always tempted to revert to his old way of hitting the ball.

_____ 18. "Lots of kids flunked" is a colloquial expression for "Many students failed."

SED, SID, SESS—to sit

If you have a **sedentary** job, you probably *sit* at a desk all day. If you work **assiduously**, you literally *sit* at your work until it is finished. And if you have an **insidious** habit, it is one that does not seem very bad at first but that *sits* in wait for you, ready to become more and more harmful.

assess (uh ses') [AD to + SESS to sit]—*lit.* to sit near to a judge (as an assistant); to estimate the value of property for taxation. *Their property was assessed at a higher rate than formerly.*

assessor (uh ses' ur) [AD to + SESS to sit]—*lit.* one who sits near to a judge as an assistant; an official who assesses property for taxation. *They were waiting for the assessor to evaluate their new home.*

assiduous (uh sij' o͞o us)—*lit.* sitting at something until it is finished; persistent. *The new clerk was assiduous in performing all his duties.*

insidious (in sid' ē us) [IN in + SID to sit]—*lit.* sitting in wait for; treacherous, more dangerous than seems evident. *Malaria is an insidious disease, remaining in the body ready to strike again and again.*

obsess (ub ses') [OB against + SESS to sit]—*lit.* to sit against; to besiege like an evil spirit; to preoccupy the mind abnormally. *He was obsessed with the fear of failure.*

obsession (ub sesh' un) [OB against + SESS to sit]—originally, the act of an evil spirit in ruling (sitting against) one; now, a persistent idea, desire, or emotion that cannot be got rid of by reasoning. *Her desire to get into the movies had become an obsession.*

preside (pri zīd') [PRE before + SID to sit]—*lit.* to sit before a meeting to conduct it. *The vice president had to preside in the president's absence.*

president (prez' ud unt) [PRE before + SID to sit]—*lit.* one who sits before a group as its head. *We waited for the president to state his views.*

sedative (sed' uh tiv)—*lit.* a medicine that makes one sit down or quiet down; a medicine that calms nervousness or excitement. *The doctor prescribed a sedative to calm him.*

sedentary (sed' n ter ē)—requiring much sitting. *Because he had a sedentary job, he didn't get enough exercise.*

sediment (sed' uh munt)—material that sits at the bottom of a liquid, as the sediment in a stream. *We noted the sediment in the bottom of the glass.*

session (sesh' un)—the sitting together of a group. *School is in session now.*

siege (sēj)—*lit.* sitting down before a town with the intention of capturing it; a prolonged attack, as of illness. *She had a siege of flu that lasted all winter.*

subside (sub sīd') [SUB under + SID to sit]—*lit.* to sit under; to sink to a lower level; to settle down. *After midnight the noise subsided.*

subsidiary (sub sid′ ē er ē) [SUB under + SID to sit]—*lit.* sitting under; serving to assist or supplement; subordinate. *The company had several subsidiary branches.*

subsidy (sub′ suh dē) [SUB under + SID to sit]—*lit.* sitting under prices to hold them up; government financial support. *When corn prices were low, the farmers received a subsidy.*

supersede (sōō pur sēd′) [SUPER above + SED to sit]—*lit.* to sit above; to take the place of; to displace. *Solar heating is superseding other forms of heating in many areas.*

ALSO: dissident, reside, residue, sedan

☐**EXERCISE 1** Write the appropriate SED, SID, SESS word.

1. A _____ occupation had never appealed to her because she didn't like to sit still.

2. Nevertheless she was an _____ worker, doing the job to the best of her ability.

3. The government _____ to farmers was cut back during the depression.

4. The chemicals had an _____ effect on the stream, the real damage not showing up for months.

5. The complaints of the environmentalists about the situation did not

   _____ when the election was over.

6. The word processor has _____ the typewriter.

7. Having everything immaculate is an _____ with her.

8. The company's _____ offices were located overseas where labor was cheaper.

9. Becoming _____ with a desire to win, he thought of nothing else.

10. What he has done for the school is so important that it would be difficult to

    _____ its value.

11. The county _____ evaluated their land.

SPEC, SPIC, SPECT—to look

In ancient Rome certain men were appointed to *look* at the flight of birds for omens or signs. The kind of birds, their position in the sky, and the direction of their flight determined whether the time was **auspicious** [AVI bird + SPIC to look] for any new undertaking. The term auspicious came to mean "full of good omens," and still today we speak of an auspicious time to ask a favor or to suggest a new policy.

aspect (as' pekt) [AD to + SPECT to look]—the way something looks from a certain point of view. *He was concerned about another aspect of the case.*

auspicious (aw spish' us) [AVI bird + SPIC to look]—originally, looking at the flight of birds for omens; today, promising good luck; favorable. *It wasn't an auspicious time to ask for a raise.*

conspicuous (kun spik' yuh wus) [CON (intensive) + SPIC to look]—easy to notice (look at); obvious. *Her late arrival made her conspicuous.*

despicable (duh spik' uh bul) [DE down + SPIC to look]—looked down on; deserving to be despised; contemptible. *Reading someone else's mail is despicable.*

expect (ik spekt') [EX out + SPECT to look]—to look out for; to anticipate. *I expect to hear from him soon.*

inspect (in spekt') [IN into + SPECT to look]—to look into carefully. *We waited for the border guard to inspect our luggage.*

introspection (in truh spek' shun) [INTRO within + SPECT to look]—a looking within one's own mind. *Introspection was valuable in helping her solve some of her problems.*

perspective (pur spek' tiv) [PER through + SPECT to look]—the ability to look at things in their true relationship; point of view. *Whether you consider the difficulty insurmountable depends on your perspective.*

perspicacious (per spi kā' shus) [PER through + SPIC to look]—having the ability to look through something and understand it; perceptive. *In dealing with individual employee problems, he was exceptionally perspicacious.*

prospect (prah' spekt) [PRO forward + SPECT to look]—a looking forward; the outlook for something, as a prospect for a good crop. *The prospect for lower taxes is slim.*

respect (ri spekt') [RE again + SPECT to look]—*lit.* to look on again; to look on with regard or esteem. *We have the greatest respect for our leader.*

retrospect (ret' ruh spekt) [RETRO backward + SPECT to look]—a looking backward. *In retrospect his life did not seem so unhappy.*

specious (spē' shus)—looking good on first sight but actually not so. *It was hard not to be taken in by the specious advertising for curing baldness.*

specter (spec'tur)—a mental image that looks real; a ghost; any object of fear or dread. *Her father was troubled by the specter of unemployment.*

spectrum (spek' trum)—a series of colored bands seen when light passes through a prism. *All the colors of the spectrum were included in her painting.* Also, a broad range of ideas or activities. *His interests included the entire spectrum of the arts.*

speculate (spek' yuh lāt)—*lit.* to look at; to reflect on or ponder. *The candidate speculated on his chances of winning.*

suspect (sus pekt') [SUB under + SPECT to look]—to look under outward appearances; to regard with suspicion. *I suspect they have selfish motives.*

ALSO: circumspect, inauspicious, introspective, perspicacity, prospective, prospector, prospectus, respectable, retrospection, species, specific, specimen, spectacle, spectacles, spectacular, spectator, suspicious

---

□**EXERCISE 1** Write the appropriate SPEC, SPIC, SPECT word.

1. The failure of the first project was not an _____ start for the coming year.

2. The salesperson could see the problem from the customer's _____.

3. She enjoyed living those years again in _____.

4. He examined his motives in a moment of quiet _____.

5. Cheating the person who had befriended him was _____.

6. The professor was unusually _____ in analyzing the problems of the students.

7. The _____ advertising made the car deal look like a giveaway.

8. In that play one experiences the entire _____ of emotions.

9. The _____ of failure haunted her.

10. The golf pro wouldn't _____ on the outcome of the U.S. Open.

SUB—under

Prisoners in Roman times were forced to crawl *under* a yoke (like the yoke put on oxen) formed from three spears, thus showing that from that time forward they were the subjects of their conquerors. They were brought *under* (SUB) the yoke (JUGUM) or **subjugated**. We still use the word subjugate today to mean subdue or make **subservient**.

Many SUB words are easy to understand when we know that SUB means *under:* **subcommittee, subconscious, subcontractor, subculture, subnormal, substandard,** and **subway.** But SUB can also help clarify the meaning of some less common words such as **subliminal** and **subsume.**

subject (accent on last syllable) (sub jekt') [SUB under + JECT to throw]— *lit.* to throw under the influence of; to submit to the authority of, as to subject oneself to a strict diet. *She learned to subject herself to the office routine.*

> (There is also, of course, **subject** with the accent on the first syllable. *Her favorite subject is math.*)

subjugate (sub' juh gāt) [SUB under + JUGUM a yoke]—*lit.* to place under a yoke; to conquer. *The invaders subjugated the primitive tribe.*

subliminal (sub lim' uh nul) [SUB under + LIMIN threshold]—below the threshold of conscious perception. *The popcorn ad flashed on the theater screen too briefly to be seen consciously, but it had a subliminal effect because people immediately started going to the lobby for popcorn.*

submerge (sub murj') [SUB under + MERG to plunge]—to plunge under water. *I learned to swim a few strokes when completely submerged.*

submit (sub mit') [SUB under + MIT to send]—to put (send) oneself under the authority of. *I had to submit to the rules.*

subpoena (suh pē' nuh) [SUB under + POENA penalty (the first two words of the order)]—a legal order requiring a person to appear in court to give testimony. *She received a subpoena to appear in court the next week.*

sub rosa (sub rō' zuh) [SUB under + ROS rose]—*lit.* under the rose (from an ancient custom of hanging a rose over the council table to indicate that all present were sworn to secrecy); in confidence. *In the interview the president was speaking sub rosa.*

subservient (sub sur' vē unt) [SUB under + SERV to serve]—*lit.* serving under someone; submissive, as a servant might be. *His attitude toward his superiors was always subservient.*

subsistence (sub sis' tunts)—*lit.* underexistence; the barest means to sustain life. *They had barely enough food for subsistence.*

subsume (sub sōōm') [SUB under + SUM to take]—to include under a more general category. *The three minor rules are subsumed under the major one.*

subterfuge (sub' tur fyōoj) [SUB under + FUG to flee]—*lit.* fleeing under cover; an action used to avoid an unpleasant situation. *By using the subterfuge of having to work overtime, he avoided going to the meeting.*

subterranean (sub tuh rā' nē un) [SUB under + TERR earth]—under the surface of the earth. *Subterranean remains of an early civilization were found on the island.*

subversive (sub vur' siv) [SUB under + VERS to turn]—*lit.* to turn under; tending to undermine or overthrow. *The government was threatened by subversive groups.*

ALSO: subcutaneous, subjective, submarine, submit, subordinate, subscribe, subsequent, subside, subsidy, subtle, suburb, suffuse, surreptitious, suspect

---

☐**EXERCISE 1**   Write the appropriate SUB word.

1. He was completely _____ by the giant wave.

2. The prison inmates were _____ to strict rules.

3. With such a low-paying job, he and his family lived at a _____ level.

4. The dictator was trying to quell the _____ forces in the country.

5. She thought of a clever _____ to get out of doing the job.

6. He was so _____ that he never objected to his supervisor's unreasonable demands.

7. The superpower was trying to _____ all the small nations around it.

8. A person can be influenced not only in conscious ways but also in _____ ways.

9. Actually all his other arguments can be _____ under his one main argument.

10. The driver of the other car received a _____ to appear in court as a witness.

11. Bats flew out of the _____ cave.

12. Unwilling to have his remarks published, the dean asked that they be considered _____.

SUPER—above, over

How do you describe people who raise their eyebrows and look down on others in a haughty way? Two roots—SUPER *above* and CILIUM *eyelid*—combined to form the Latin word *supercilium* meaning eyebrow. And eventually anyone who raised the eyebrows in a haughty way came to be called a **supercilious** person, a raised-eyebrows person.

insuperable (in sōō′ pur uh bul) [IN not + SUPER over]—not capable of being overcome. *His height was an insuperable barrier to his becoming a jockey.*

soprano (su pran′ ō)—one having a voice range above other voices. *Her soprano solo won top honors.*

superb (su purb′)—above ordinary quality; excellent. *That was a superb performance.*

supercilious (sōō pur sil′ ē us) [SUPER above + CILIUM eyelid]—*lit.* above the eyelid; eyebrows raised in a haughty way. *She cast a supercilious glance at the person who had dared to disagree with her.*

superfluous (su pur′ flu wus) [SUPER over + FLU to flow]—*lit.* overflowing what is needed; extra. *The essay was full of superfluous words.*

superimpose (sōō pur im pōz′)—to lay something over something else. *The modern painting had been superimposed on an old masterpiece.*

superior (su pir′ ē ur)—above others. *Our home team was superior.*

supernumerary (sōō pur nōō′ muh rer ē) [SUPER above + NUMER number]—someone in excess of (above) the number required; an extra. *Since she was given no work to do, she felt like a supernumerary.* Also, a performer in the theater without a speaking part. *He was a supernumerary in the mob scene.*

supersonic (sōō pur son′ ik) [SUPER above + SON sound]—above the speed of sound. *Supersonic planes cause the sound known as sonic boom.*

superstition (sōō pur stish′ un) [SUPER above + STA to stand]—*lit.* a belief standing above other beliefs; a belief that is inconsistent with the known laws of science. *Believing that the number 13 is unlucky is a superstition.*

supervise (soo′ pur viz) [SUPER over + VIS to see]—to oversee others. *She will supervise the preschoolers.*

supervisor (soo′ pur vi zur) [SUPER over + VIS to see]—one who oversees others. *She is the supervisor of the preschool.*

supreme (su prēm′)—above all others; highest in rank. *He considers himself the supreme authority in that company.*

surplus (sur′ plus) [SUPER above + PLUS more]—*lit.* above more; above what is needed. *We have a surplus of volunteers.*

ALSO: superabundant, superannuated, superhuman, superintend, supernatural, supersede

---

☐**EXERCISE 1** What word would take the place of each definition?

1. above the speed of sound   _____

2. more than is needed   _____

3. to lay something over something else   _____

4. incapable of being overcome   _____

5. haughty   _____

☐**EXERCISE 2 REVIEW** As a review of the words you've been studying, read these paragraphs. How many of the ten words do you know without looking them up?

A town meeting was called to consider a lumber company's proposal to cut trees in a town-owned woodland. The proponents of the plan claimed it would create jobs and bring unprecedented wealth to the town, which was in chronic economic depression. They said that those trying to circumvent the plan were asking for the demise of the community.

Those interested in ecology, on the other hand, said that the natural beauty of the area would be spoiled and that several endemic plants might become extinct. It isn't possible, they said, to equate financial gain with the good life.

The problem seemed insuperable because after three hours of discussion, no consensus was reached.

☐**EXERCISE 3** Can you add a few more words to your root chain—or start a new one?

SYN, SYM, SYL—together, with

Among the ancient Greeks, a **symposium** was a *drinking together* party [SYM together + POS to drink], especially after a banquet. Through the years the meaning has changed until today a symposium is no longer a drinking party but a meeting or conference at which several speakers come *together* to deliver opinions on a certain topic.

In preceding pages we have seen that the root SYN, SYM, SYL means *together* in such words as **symmetrical, sympathy, symphony,** and **synchronize.** Whether the word will begin with SYN, SYM, or SYL often depends on what letter follows. For instance, it would be difficult to pronounce SYNmetrical; therefore SYN becomes SYM. For more about how a root may change one of its letters for easier pronunciation, see page 6.

syllogism (sil' uh jiz um) [SYL together + LOG word]—*lit.* words together; a form of argument or reasoning consisting of two statements and a conclusion drawn from them. *Here is an example of a syllogism: All mammals are warm-blooded; whales are mammals; therefore whales are warm-blooded.*

symbol (sim' bul) [SYM together + BOL to throw]—*lit.* things thrown together for comparison; something that represents something else. *Diamonds are a symbol of wealth.*

symposium (sim pō' zē um) [SYM together + POS to drink]—originally, a drinking (together) party following a banquet among the early Greeks; now, a meeting at which several speakers deliver opinions on a certain topic. *A symposium on the use of national parks was held in Washington, D.C.*

synagogue (sin' u gahg) [SYN together + AGOG to lead]—a place where Jewish people are led together for worship. *We visited an architecturally famous synagogue in Elkins Park, Pennsylvania.*

syndrome (sin' drōm) [SYN together + DROM to run]—*lit.* a running together; a group of symptoms that run together and indicate a specific disease or condition. *He had the usual flu syndrome: sore throat, headache, and aching muscles.*

synergistic (sin ur jis' tik) [SYN together + ERG work]—working together, as when the joint action of two drugs increases the effectiveness of each. *Certain drugs when taken together are synergistic. The two playwrights had a synergistic relationship, each working more effectively when they worked together.*

synod (sin' ud) [SYN together + OD road, journey]—*lit.* a journey together; a council or assembly, especially of church officials. *The church synod met in a different city each year.*

synopsis (su nahp′ sus) [SYN together + OP sight]—*lit.* a seeing things together; a brief general summary. *Before beginning our study of the novel, we read a synopsis of it.*

syntax (sin′ tax) [SYN together + TAX arrangement]—the way words are arranged together to form sentences. *Because English was a second language for her, she often had trouble with syntax.* Also, in computer science, the rules governing the construction of any computer language. *The computer kept responding, "Syntax error."*

synthesis (sin′ thuh sis) [SYN together + THES to put]—*lit.* a putting together; the combining of separate elements into a whole. *Sandburg said that poetry is a synthesis of hyacinths and biscuits.*

synthetic (sin thet′ ik) [SYN together + THET to put]—*lit.* put together; produced by putting separate elements together; artificial. *Instead of a synthetic cloth, she wanted a natural fiber such as silk or cotton.*

ALSO: asymmetric, photosynthesis, symbiosis, symbiotic, symmetrical, sympathy, symphony, synchronize, synergy, synonym

---

☐**EXERCISE 1**   Write the appropriate SYN, SYM, SYL word.

1. The final motion was a _____ of all their ideas.

2. Six speakers were scheduled for the _____ on air pollution.

3. _____ cloth is made by combining various chemical elements.

4. The diagnosis was simple because the child had the typical chickenpox

   _____.

5. The matter was discussed at the annual meeting of the church _____.

6. Because he had never paid any attention to grammar in high school, he now

   had difficulty using correct _____ in his writing.

7. Learning the correct form for a _____ helped her to think logically.

8. She and her husband had a _____ relationship, each working better on the project when they worked together.

9. In an early chapter of *The Grapes of Wrath,* Steinbeck uses a turtle as a

   _____ of the migrants.

TELE—far

Any word containing TELE will have *far* in its meaning. Such words as **telephone** and **telegraph** and **television** have become so common that we say them without thinking what they really mean.

telegraph (tel' uh graf) [TELE far + GRAPH to write]—*lit.* an instrument for far writing; a system for transmitting messages by electric impulses sent through a wire or converted into radio waves. *Western Union offices were originally called telegraph offices.*

telemetry (tuh lem' uh trē) [TELE far + METER measure]—the automatic measurement and transmission of data by radio from far away, as from space vehicles to a receiving station. *Reports of the weather on Mars came to the research center in California by telemetry.*

telepathy (tuh lep' uh thē) [TELE far + PATH feeling]—*lit.* far feeling; the supposed communication between two people far apart by other than normal sensory means. *Because they so often thought of the same thing at the same time, they were convinced it was telepathy.*

telephone (tel' uh fōn) [TELE far + PHON sound]—an instrument for transmitting sounds from far away. *Alexander Graham Bell invented the telephone.*

telescope (tel' uh skōp) [TELE far + SCOP to look]—an instrument for looking at far objects. *We looked at the moon through a telescope.*

television (tel' uh vizh un) [TELE far + VIS to see]—an instrument for seeing images from afar. *Television was unknown in the first part of the twentieth century.*

ALSO: telecommunication, telegram, telephoto

☐EXERCISE 1 REVIEW Write C in front of each sentence in which all words are used correctly. No answers are provided at the back of the book for this exercise.

_____ 1. The flood subsided before too much damage was done.

_____ 2. In retrospect she realized how many wrong decisions she had made.

_____ 3. We are looking for a specious house, one with at least ten rooms.

_____ 4. Not until the water recedes will there be good shell collecting along the beach.

_____ 5. We found that the problem was insuperable and could easily be solved with a little effort.

_____ 6. The kindergarten children were learning to read by the phonics method.

_____ 7. He received his pedigree at the spring convocation.

_____ 8. The enemy projectile just missed the city.

_____ 9. It seemed like an auspicious time to present the new bill to the voters.

_____ 10. The director tried to influence the board members, but they were recalcitrant.

_____ 11. He ascribed his success to hard work and a bit of luck.

_____ 12. The candidate was assiduous in canvassing every house in the district.

_____ 13. The hostess cast a supercilious glance at the guest who arrived in jeans.

_____ 14. The police were on a tour of introspection in the neighborhood.

_____ 15. To proscribe is to write a prescription for medicine.

_____ 16. She was moved to tears by the pathos in the story.

_____ 17. Remiss means to miss again.

_____ 18. He was attempting to influence his distant son through telepathy.

_____ 19. The old manuscript had been copied and illustrated by scribes.

_____ 20. The play ended with a prologue by the hero.

_____ 21. All my arguments can be subsumed under one main argument.

_____ 22. They had their property assessed for tax purposes.

_____ 23. For the mob scene in the movie, hundreds of supernumeraries were hired.

_____ 24. They walked over to the syndrome to watch the football practice.

_____ 25. The microwave oven has now superseded the conventional oven.

_____ 26. A few of the late author's unpublished poems have been found and are now being published posthumously.

TORT—to twist

If you are driving along a little-traveled mountain road, you will certainly understand the meaning of **tortuous**. It comes from the root TORT *to twist* and means full of *twists* and turns. You can speak of a tortuous road, a tortuous path through the woods, a tortuous climb down a mountain, a tortuous career with advances and reverses all along the way, or tortuous arguments that wander all over rather than moving directly toward a goal. Tortuous may also mean morally *twisted*, deceitful, not straightforward. Tortuous explanations may *twist* the truth, and tortuous deals may be *twisted* or crooked.

Tortuous must not be confused with **torturous,** which is related to torture and means inflicting physical or mental pain.

contortionist (kun tawr' shun ist) [CON together + TORT to twist]—an acrobat who can twist the body and limbs into extraordinary positions. *At the circus we watched an expert contortionist.*

distort (dis tawrt') [DIS away + TORT to twist]—*lit.* to twist away; to twist from the true meaning, as to distort the facts. *Her description of the accident distorted the facts.*

extort (ik stawrt') [EX out + TORT to twist]—*lit.* to twist something out; to obtain by violence or threat. *They tried to extort money by blackmail.*

retort (ri tawrt') [RE back + TORT to twist]—*lit.* a twisting back on the giver; a reply to an insult or a criticism. *His retort to her criticism was shattering.*

torch (tawrch)—a portable light produced by a flammable material twisted around the end of a stick and ignited (early torches were made of twisted flax dipped in tallow). *We watched the torchlight parade.*

torment (tawr ment')—*lit.* to twist; to annoy. *Along the shore the mosquitoes tormented us.*

tort (tawrt)—*lit.* a twisted action; a wrongful act, injury, or damage for which a civil suit can be brought for damages. *If a person breaks a shop window, that person has committed a tort against the shop owner.*

tortoise (tawr' tus)—a turtle, especially a land turtle, so called perhaps because of its twisted feet. *The waitress worked at the speed of a tortoise.*

tortuous (tawrch' uh wus)—full of twists and turns. *Drive cautiously because that's a tortuous road.* Also, not straightforward; deceitful. *Her tortuous dealings gave her the reputation of being untrustworthy.*

torture (tawr' chur)—any severe physical or mental pain. *Waiting for the judges' decision after the contest was torture.*

torturous (tawrch' uh rus)—inflicting physical or mental pain. *The defendant had to undergo torturous questioning.*

ALSO: contortion, torque, torsion

118

☐EXERCISE 1 Write the appropriate TORT word.

1. By threatening to resign she tried to _____ a promise of promotion.
2. With a clever _____ to the insult, he managed to change the subject.
3. The audience was amazed at the acrobatic performance of the _____.

4. Emphasizing unimportant details, she tried to _____ the case.
5. The judge branded the defendant's questionable dealings with the loan

    company as _____.

6. I spent a _____ morning having a wisdom tooth pulled.

7. The civil suit regarding that _____ was settled out of court.

☐EXERCISE 2 REVIEW Write C in front of each sentence in which all words are used correctly.

_____ 1. The posterior legs of an animal are its front legs.
_____ 2. The Preamble to the Constitution begins with the words "We the people of the United States, in order to form a more perfect Union. . . ."
_____ 3. The small nation refused to be subjugated by its powerful neighbor.
_____ 4. Although she did not appear ill, her friends knew she was suffering from an insidious disease.
_____ 5. By a clever subterfuge, he avoided taking part in the debate.
_____ 6. Her proclivity toward revealing trade secrets cost her her job.
_____ 7. The subpoena released him from jail.
_____ 8. The speaker claimed that the tax reform would be a panacea for all the ills of the country.
_____ 9. She was malignant when she heard that she had been fired.
_____ 10. Always a sedate person, she kicked off her shoes and sat down on the floor.
_____ 11. The apathy of the committee precluded their accomplishing much.
_____ 12. Preeminent in her field, she was also knowledgeable in several others.
_____ 13. Most of the work in that company is done not in the main office but in the subsidiary offices.
_____ 14. Everyone commiserated with him when he lost the match.
_____ 15. We were amazed at her perfidious actions toward a company that had treated her well through the years.
_____ 16. The department of meteorology is predicting an early spring.

TRI—three

Like UNI (one) and BI (two), TRI is easy to spot at the beginning of many words, but knowing the roots that follow often gives the words new meaning. And sometimes a TRI word has a long history. For example, **tribe** originally referred to one of the *three* groups into which the Roman people were divided.

triangle (trī′ ang gul)—a plane figure having three sides and three angles. *I learned about triangles in my geometry course.*

tribe (trīb)—originally, one of the three groups into which the Romans were divided; now, a group of people united by the same race and customs. *We bought some blankets from an Indian tribe.*

trident (trīd′ unt) [TRI three + DENT tooth]—a long three-pronged (toothed) spear. *Neptune, the Roman god of the sea, is usually pictured holding a trident.*

triennial (trī en′ ē ul) [TRI three + ENN year]—occurring every three years. *The society held a triennial convention.*

trilateral (trī lat′ ur ul) [TRI three + LATER side]—having three sides. *The three countries signed a trilateral treaty.*

trilingual (trī ling′ gwul) [TRI three + LINGU language]—speaking three languages. *In Switzerland many people are trilingual, speaking German, French, and Italian.*

trilogy (tril′ uh jē)—three literary, dramatic, or musical compositions that, though each is complete in itself, make a related series. *Last year I read all three books of Tolkien's trilogy* The Lord of the Rings.

Trinity (trin′ uh tē)—a set of three persons or things that form a unit, as the three divine persons of Christian theology. *The Apostles' Creed affirms belief in the Trinity.*

trio (trē′ ō)—any three people or things joined or associated. *The men's trio sang a concluding number.*

tripartite (trī pahr′ tīt)—composed of three parts; shared by three parties. *The three countries made a tripartite agreement.*
(Trilateral and tripartite are close synonyms.)

triplets (trip′ luts)—three children born at one birth. *The birth of triplets was a great surprise to the family.*

triplicate (trip′ li kut) [TRI three + PLIC to fold]—threefold; one of three identical copies or things. *The boss asked for the letters in triplicate.*

tripod (trī′ pahd) [TRI three + POD foot]—a three-legged stand for supporting a camera or other instrument. *Our telescope stood on a tripod.*

trivet (triv′ it)—a three-legged stand for holding a vessel or dish. *The hot dish stood on a small black trivet on a side table.*

ALSO: trigonometry, trinomial, trivia, trivial

□EXERCISE 1 What TRI word names the following?

1. The three divine persons of Christian theology _____

2. a three-legged stand _____ or _____

3. a long three-pronged spear _____

4. three literary compositions in a series _____

What TRI word describes the following?

5. speaking three languages _____

6. held every three years _____

7. shared by three countries _____ or _____

□EXERCISE 2   REVIEW   Write C in front of each sentence in which all words are used correctly.

_____ 1. Punctuating a sentence incorrectly can distort its meaning.

_____ 2. Her kitchen contained a full panoply of modern equipment.

_____ 3. The speaker was smartly dressed in a nondescript outfit.

_____ 4. His unpleasant retort may precipitate a quarrel.

_____ 5. Her path to fame had been tortuous, with many wins and many losses.

_____ 6. Living like a recluse, he enjoyed chatting with his neighbors.

_____ 7. We had fun wandering through that subterranean cave.

_____ 8. The captors tried to extort a confession from their captive.

_____ 9. Despite his protuberant belly, he still munches chocolate bars.

_____ 10. It was a long, torturous road down the mountain.

_____ 11. Anyone with a sedentary job is sure to get plenty of exercise.

_____ 12. Telemetry has enabled us to discover many facts about Mars.

_____ 13. The doctor was unusually perspicacious in diagnosing the illness.

_____ 14. The child was precocious but had a profusion of emotional problems.

_____ 15. The ads flashing on the screen for seconds had a subliminal effect on the viewers.

_____ 16. Their report was a synthesis of the ideas that had been presented at the symposium.

_____ 17. The director was given profuse praise by the grateful cast.

_____ 18. Preponderant in my mind was the necessity of saving that forest from the developers.

VER—true

If you doubt someone's **veracity**, you doubt that person's *truthfulness*. If you speak of a **veritable** downpour of rain, you mean that it was *truly* a downpour. To **verify** something is to prove that it is *true*. When jury members give a **verdict** [VER true + DICT to speak], they are literally speaking the **truth**. Even the little word **very** comes from VER and means *truly*.

veracious (vuh rā′ shus)—truthful; accurate. *The newspaper gave a veracious account of the incident.*

veracity (vuh ras′ uh tē)—truthfulness. *No one doubted her veracity.*

verdict (vur′ dikt) [VER true + DICT to speak]—*lit.* a speaking of the truth; the decision of a jury. *The jury gave their verdict of not guilty.*

verifiable (ver′ uh fī uh bul)—capable of being proved true. *None of his statements were verifiable.*

verification (ver ruh fuh kā′ shun)—establishment of the truth. *Before cashing the check, the clerk asked for verification of the customer's identity.*

verify (ver′ u fī)—to prove something is true. *I can verify all the figures in my account.*

verily (ver′ uh lē)—an archaic word meaning truly. *"Verily, I say unto you" is a common expression in the Bible.*

veritable (ver′ uh tuh bul)—true; actual. *He was a veritable Good Samaritan.*

verity (ver′ uh tē)—a statement, principle, or belief that is considered to be established truth, as religious verities. *Alone on the mountain, he had time to ponder the external verities.*

very (ver′ ē)—truly, absolutely. *Limit your use of very in your compositions.*

ALSO: aver, verisimilitude

☐**EXERCISE 1**　Write the appropriate VER word.

1. With her amazing knowledge of facts, she's a _____ encyclopedia.

2. He'd never lie to you; you can depend on his _____.

3. I was careful to _____ each fact before presenting it.

4. The travel agent asked for _____ of the child's age.

5. You can count on her to give a _____ report of the trial because she always tells the truth.

6. Little _____ evidence could be obtained about the accident because there had been no witnesses.

7. He was now questioning some of the _____ he had always accepted in his youth.

☐**EXERCISE 2 REVIEW** Underline the appropriate word.

1. Their (assiduous, insidious) tactics misled their clients.
2. My sister has a (phobic, endemic) dread of air travel.
3. The dean suspected that there were (subversive, subsistence) activities going on in the dorms.
4. Because of his (xenophobia, photophobia) he had to avoid strong sunlight.
5. The police (proscribed, ascribed) the accident to drunken driving.
6. The (veracity, verdict) of the witness was never questioned.
7. The clear skies (preclude, presage) a pleasant day.
8. The contestant was (assessed, obsessed) with a desire to succeed.
9. Because I liked the first volume, I wanted to read the rest of the (trilogy, trinity).
10. The casserole stood on a small (trident, trivet) on the dining room table.
11. One group has a yearly meeting, and the other has a (triennial, trilateral) meeting.
12. The view from the (promontory, proclivity) was inspiring.
13. The Hebrews practiced (monotheism, pantheism).
14. Pencils are made from (graphite, graffiti).
15. The three countries signed a (tripartite, triennial) arms agreement.

VERT, VERS—to turn

A **verse** or line of poetry comes from the root VERS *to turn*. Just as a plow makes a furrow and then at the end of the furrow *turns* to make another parallel one, so a verse of poetry *turns* when it comes to the end of the line and goes back to make another line.

Universe also comes from the root VERS. It is made up of UNI *one* and VERS *to turn* and means literally all things that exist *turned* into one. The ancients thought all the heavenly bodies were *turning* around the earth, *turning* into one whole.

adversary (ad′ vur ser ē) [AD against + VERS to turn]—*lit.* one turned against another; opponent. *She easily defeated her adversary in the contest.*

adverse (ad vurs′) [AD against + VERS to turn]—turned against; unfavorable. *The company had to cope with adverse publicity.*

adversity (ad vur′ suh tē) [AD against + VERS to turn]—the state of being turned against; misfortune. *His years of adversity made him sympathetic to others in trouble.*

advertise (ad vur tīz′) [AD to + VERT to turn]—to turn attention to. *I'm going to advertise my bike for sale.*

averse (uh vurs′) [AB from + VERS to turn]—*lit.* to turn from; having a feeling of great distaste. *Having lost so much money on the lottery, she was averse to risking any more.*

aversion (uh vur′ zhun) [AB away + VERS to turn]—*lit.* a turning away; extreme dislike. *Because of her aversion to work, she never held a job long.*

avert (uh vurt′) [AB away + VERT to turn]—to turn away. *She averted her eyes from the unpleasant scene.* Also, to prevent. *By taking preventive measures, they hope to avert another disaster.*

controversy (kahn′ truh vur sē) [CONTRA against + VERS to turn]—*lit.* opinions turned against each other; a dispute. *The controversy over the use of the land remained unsettled.*

convert (kun vurt′) [CON together + VERT to turn]—*lit.* to turn together to the same belief; to turn from one belief to another. *They tried to convert me to their political beliefs.*

divert (duh vurt′) [DI away + VERT to turn]—to turn away, as to turn someone's attention away from something. *I tried to listen to the lecture, but the whispering behind me diverted my attention.*

inadvertent (in ud vur′ tunt) [IN not + AD to + VERT to turn]—*lit.* not turning one's mind to a matter; unintentional. *He made an inadvertent reference to the plans for the surprise party.*

introvert (in′ truh vurt) [INTRO within + VERT to turn]—*lit.* one who turns within; one whose thoughts and interests are directed inward. *Introverts think mainly about themselves.*

obverse (ob vurs') [OB toward + VERS to turn]—turned toward the observer; the side bearing the main design (as opposed to reverse). *The obverse side of a U.S. coin bears the main design and the date.*

perverse (pur vurs') [PER (intensive) + VERS to turn]—turned away from what is right or good; obstinately disobedient or difficult. *Always perverse, he opposed the wishes of the group.*

universe (yoo' nuh vurs) [UNI one + VERS to turn]—*lit.* all things that exist turned into one; everything in the heavens turned into one whole. *I'm learning about the universe in my astronomy course.*

versatile (vur' suh tul)—able to turn easily from one subject or occupation to another; competent in many fields. *An unusually versatile actor, he is able to play any role from hero to clown.*

verse (vurs) [VERS to turn]—*lit.* turning from one line to the next in poetry, like a plow turning to make parallel furrows. *I wrote a verse for my Christmas cards this year.*

version (vur' zhun) [VERS to turn]—a translation or turning of one language into another, as a version of Homer; an account related from a specific point of view, as a version of an accident. *My brother's version of the accident and mine differed.*

vertebra (vur' tuh bruh)—a bone of the spinal column that turns. *A vertebra is one of 20 short, thick bones through which the spinal cord runs.*

ALSO: anniversary, averse, converse, conversion, convertible, diverse, diversify, diversion, divorce, extrovert, incontrovertible, inverse, invertebrate, revert, subversive, versus (vs.), vertigo

---

☐**EXERCISE 1**　Write the appropriate VERT, VERS word.

1. I'd rather have him as a partner than as an _____ in the game.
2. Instead of saying, "Heads or tails?" he always said, "_____ or reverse?"
3. I regretted having made an _____ reference to her previous job.
4. Spending much time analyzing his thoughts, he was a true _____.
5. Completely disillusioned, he was _____ to giving any money to the project.
6. No matter what I want, he is always _____ and wants the opposite.
7. During that year of _____, he lost his job and his home.
8. Our trip had to be postponed because of _____ weather.
9. When I glanced at her, she _____ her eyes.

10. My sister is a _____ person, equally good at tennis, oil painting, and cooking.

11. An _____ to a particular food can sometimes be traced to an allergy.

☐**EXERCISE 2　REVIEW**　Give the meaning of each root and a word in which it is found.

	MEANING	WORD
1. PHON		
2. POST		
3. PRE		
4. PRO		
5. RE		
6. SCRIB, SCRIPT		
7. SED, SID, SESS		
8. SPEC, SPIC, SPECT		
9. SUB		
10. SUPER		
11. SYN, SYM, SYL		
12. TELE		
13. TORT		
14. TRI		
15. VER		
16. VERT, VERS		

☐EXERCISE 3 REVIEW The 12 underlined words are ones you've studied. Copy them below and give their meanings. Understanding all the words should make rereading the paragraph satisfying.

Faced in the 1980s with the prospect of chronic oil shortages, most Americans concurred that everyone must conserve. Government edicts reduced speed limits and controlled temperatures in public buildings. Individuals overcame their propensity to drive their cars to work and no longer regarded public transportation with aversion. Others experimented with a spectrum of solutions from windmills to solar power. All the efforts taken together, though not a panacea for our energy problems, were an important prologue to what we must do to make sure some oil supplies will be left for posterity. And still today we are stuggling to find ways to circumvent the unprecedented oil shortage that threatens us.

WORD	WORD MEANING
1. _____	_____
2. _____	_____
3. _____	_____
4. _____	_____
5. _____	_____
6. _____	_____
7. _____	_____
8. _____	_____
9. _____	_____
10. _____	_____
11. _____	_____
12. _____	_____

VIA—way

In Roman times a place where three roads met was called the three-*way* place or trivia (TRI three + VIA way), and when people on their way to market gathered at that place to chat about unimportant matters, their talk came to be called **trivia** or three-*way* talk. Eventually any talk about unimportant things was called **trivial**. So today, when we talk about trivial things, we are reminded of those Romans who did likewise.

deviate (dē′ vē āt) [DE from + VIA way]—to turn away from an established way. *Anyone who deviates from the rules is likely to be in trouble.*

deviation (dē vē ā′ shun) [DE from + VIA way]—a turning aside from an established way. *The chairperson would not tolerate the slightest deviation from parliamentary rules.*

devious (dē′ vē us) [DE from + VIA way]—straying from the proper way; crooked. *His fortune had been made by devious means.*

impervious (im pur′ vē us) [IN not + PER through + VIA way]—*lit.* no way through; incapable of being passed through. *The cloth was impervious to water. His mind was impervious to reason.*

obviate (ob′ vē āt) [OB against + VIA way]—*lit.* to come against something in the way and dispose of it; to prevent. *Careful planning will obviate future difficulties.*

obvious (ob′ vē us) [OB against + VIA way]—*lit.* standing against one in the way; clearly visible; evident. *What we should do was obvious.*

previous (prē′ vē us) [PRE before + VIA way]—under way beforehand. *I learned that in a previous assignment.*

trivia (triv′ ē uh) [TRI three + VIA way]—*lit.* three-way talk; originally, the commonplace matters discussed when neighborhood gossips met at the crossroads; any unimportant matters. *A knowledge of trivia is important for quiz show contestants.*

trivial (triv′ ē ul) [TRI three + VIA way]—unimportant. *She became upset over the most trivial things.*

via (vī′ uh) [VIA way]—by way of. *We are going via Chicago.*

viaduct (vī′ uh dukt) [VIA way + DUC to lead]—a bridge leading a road (way) over a valley. *The viaduct takes the road over the railroad tracks.*

☐**EXERCISE 1   REVIEW**   Write C in front of each sentence in which all words are used correctly.

_____ 1. A rabbit chasing a dog would be preposterous.

_____ 2. I have a predilection for anything red and always try to avoid that color.

_____ 3. Morpheus was so called because he was the god of the forms that sleepers see in their dreams.

_____ 4. The coin collector turned the coin over to look at the obverse side.

_____ 5. To get her driver's license she had to give verification of her age.

_____ 6. A true introvert, he went out of his way to make friends.

_____ 7. I wasn't thinking when I made that inadvertent remark.

_____ 8. Always a versatile person, she could fit into any of several jobs.

_____ 9. Having been a poor baseball player himself, he felt empathy with his son, who was having no luck in catching the ball.

_____ 10. The administration was apathetic and really working hard to further the new plan.

_____ 11. A pedigree means literally the foot of a crane because the three-line diagram used to indicate descent looks like the foot of a crane.

_____ 12. To most people it's cacophony, but I really enjoy the sounds of an orchestra tuning up.

_____ 13. She had learned to reason according to the classic syllogisms.

_____ 14. If you follow the rules, you'll obviate further trouble.

_____ 15. Her perverse attitude made her a favorite in the office.

_____ 16. His working full-time may be an impediment to his success in college.

_____ 17. As they chatted about trivia during the musical, they were impervious to the glances of those around them.

_____ 18. As soon as the winner was announced, there was pandemonium in the stands.

_____ 19. Any deviation in following the recipe may mean failure.

_____ 20. A subservient employee is usually afraid to deviate from the norm.

_____ 21. Walking home from the subway, we were caught in a veritable downpour.

_____ 22. You may depend upon her to give a veracious account of the proceedings.

_____ 23. The officer at the border asked for veracity of my citizenship.

_____ 24. She tried to divert the attention of her guests from her mischievous child.

_____ 25. My friends refused to speculate on the outcome of the election.

VOC, VOKE—to call, voice

A **convocation** [CON together + VOC to call] is a *calling* together, an assembly. It may begin with an **invocation** [IN in + VOC to call], a *calling* for divine aid; and if the convocation is a college graduation, then the graduates will be looking forward to their **vocations** or *callings*. Later, after they are settled in their jobs, they will no doubt be thinking of **avocations** or *callings* away from their jobs.

advocate (ad' vu kut) [AD to + VOC to call]—*lit.* one called to give evidence; a person who pleads on another's behalf or for a cause. *He was an advocate of free elections in his country.*

avocation (av u kā' shun) [AB away + VOC to call]—*lit.* a calling away; a diversion; a hobby. *I spend almost as much time on my avocation as on my vocation.*

convocation (kahn vu kā' shun) [CON together + VOC to call]—*lit.* a calling together; an assembly. *I hope to get my degree at the spring convocation.*

evocative (i vok' uh tiv) [E out + VOC to call]—*lit.* calling out; calling forth. *The sounds of the forest were evocative of his early camping days.*

evoke (i vōk') [E out + VOC to call]—*lit.* to call out; to call forth, as memories or feelings. *The smell of burning leaves always evoked memories of his childhood.*

invocation (in vuh kā' shun) [IN in + VOC to call]—*lit.* a calling for divine aid; an opening prayer. *The invocation was given by the dean.*

invoke (in vōk') [IN in + VOC to call]—*lit.* to call in; to call upon for aid or support. *The accused person invoked the Fifth Amendment.*

irrevocable (i rev' uh ku bul) [IN not + RE back + VOC to call]—not capable of being called back; unalterable. *His decision was irrevocable.*

provocation (prahv uh kā' shun) [PRO forth + VOC to call]—something that calls forth irritation. *That child cries at the slightest provocation.*

provoke (pruh vōk') [PRO forth + VOC to call]—to call forth; to bring about; to cause anger or irritation. *His constant complaining provokes me.*

revoke (ri vōk') [RE back + VOC to call]—to call back. *The company revoked its earlier offer.*

vocabulary (vō kab' yuh ler ē)—*lit.* the words one can speak (call). *A large vocabulary is an asset in college.*

vocation (vō kā' shun)—a calling; an occupation or profession. *Are you pleased with your choice of a vocation?*

vociferous (vō sif' ur us) [VOC voice + FER to carry]—*lit.* carrying a loud voice; noisy. *The crowd at the rally made a vociferous protest against the location of the nuclear power plant.*

ALSO: advocacy, equivocal, equivocate, provocative, vocal

☐**EXERCISE 1** Write the appropriate VOC, VOKE word.

1. The final decision of the court was _____.

2. Looking at old photographs would always _____ memories of happy times.

3. The Pilgrims _____ God's help on their journey.

4. Although he liked his vocation, it was his _____ that really interested him.

5. When the holiday was canceled, there were _____ complaints.

6. Going back to the town where he grew up was always an _____ experience.

7. The graduation ceremony began with an _____.

8. Awards were presented at the spring _____.

9. Because of the accident, his driver's license was _____.

10. She was preparing not merely for a job but for a _____.

☐**EXERCISE 2 REVIEW** Write C in front of each sentence in which all words are used correctly. Then in each remaining blank, write the word that should have been used.

_____ 1. I'm not averse to helping you with your plan.

_____ 2. Instead of going straight home they took a circuitous route.

_____ 3. The two countries made a trilateral agreement about arms limitation.

_____ 4. We were fascinated as we watched the metamorphosis of the pupa into a moth.

_____ 5. In the botany lab we dissected a flower and named all its parts.

_____ 6. We felt that the assessor gave too low an evaluation of our house.

_____ 7. Adverse road conditions made our trip unpleasant.

_____ 8. The superpower tried to subjugate the natives on the island.

_____ 9. The secretary's proclivity toward wasting time led to her dismissal.

_____ 10. The benevolence of the lodge members aided him in his time of adversity.

_____ 11. If he were more versatile, he wouldn't be limited to just one kind of job.

_____ 12. Suffering from claustrophobia, she refused to go to the top of the tower.

COMPREHENSIVE TEST A The words in this test contain the same roots as the words in the PRELIMINARY TEST on page 9. A comparison of your two scores will indicate how much the study of word roots has increased your vocabulary.

_____ 1. ambivalence A. lack of feeling B. conflicting feelings C. jealousy
D. dislike

_____ 2. misanthrophic A. doubting B. hating marriage C. hating people
D. generous

_____ 3. antithesis A. secondary theme of an essay B. failure C. climax
D. exact opposite

_____ 4. automaton A. self-government B. government by a single person
C. one who acts mechanically D. car buff

_____ 5. beneficiary A. lawyer who handles wills B. one who receives
benefits C. one who gives money to benefit others D. one who
leaves money in a will

_____ 6. synchronize A. to keep a time record B. to compose an
accompaniment C. to cause to keep time together D. to prophesy

_____ 7. circumspect A. cautious B. hardworking C. knowledgeable
D. showing respect

_____ 8. compunction A. connecting word B. compulsion C. satisfaction
about something one has done D. a slight regret

_____ 9. incredulous A. not believing readily B. believing too readily
C. lacking credit D. not trustworthy

_____ 10. cursory A. using profanity B. critical C. hateful D. hasty and
superficial

_____ 11. demagogue A. ancient tribal god B. half man and half god
C. leader who appeals to the emotions to gain power D. leader who
works for the good of the people

_____ 12. euphonious A. having a pleasant sound B. coming from a distance
C. false D. difficult to hear

_____ 13. exonerate A. to honor B. to take out objectionable parts
C. to free from blame D. to find guilty

_____ 14. eulogy A. speech by an actor alone on the stage B. explanation of
a literary passage C. speech blaming someone D. speech praising
someone

_____ 15. colloquial A. incorrect B. talkative C. conversational D. standard

_____ 16. malevolent A. kindly B. violent C. giving money to others
D. wishing evil to others

_____ 17. emissary A. traveler B. spy C. servant D. someone sent out

_____ 18. anthropomorphic A. relating to the early Stone Age B. having human characteristics C. having animal form D. changing form

_____ 19. panoply A. impressive display B. high covering C. harsh criticism D. series of games

_____ 20. apathetic A. sad B. deserving sympathy C. pitiful D. indifferent

_____ 21. expedite A. to experiment with B. to send away C. to speed the progress of D. to make clear

_____ 22. propensity A. dislike B. thoughtfulness C. belief D. natural inclination

_____ 23. sedentary A. temporary B. permanent C. requiring much sitting D. producing sediment

_____ 24. specious A. having many rooms B. seemingly good but actually not so C. reasonable D. a category of living things

_____ 25. subterfuge A. deceptive strategy B. underwater vessel C. play acting D. hatred

_____ 26. insuperable A. extraordinary B. easily overcome C. incapable of being overcome D. best of its kind

_____ 27. symbiosis A. similarity in biologic function B. similarity in evolutionary development C. living together in close relationship D. use of symbols in literature

COMPREHENSIVE TEST B   These words contain all the roots you have studied. Give the meaning of each root and the meaning of the word.

		MEANING OF ROOT	MEANING OF WORD
1. amphibian	AMPHI	_____	
	BIO	_____	_____
2. antedate	ANTE	_____	_____
3. anthropomorphic	ANTHROP	_____	
	MORPH	_____	_____
4. antibiotic	ANTI	_____	
	BIO	_____	_____
5. asymmetric	A	_____	
	SYM	_____	
	METR	_____	_____
6. autograph	AUTO	_____	
	GRAPH	_____	_____
7. benediction	BENE	_____	
	DICT	_____	_____
8. biennial	BI	_____	
	ENN	_____	_____
9. chronometer	CHRON	_____	
	METER	_____	_____
10. circumscribe	CIRCUM	_____	
	SCRIB	_____	_____
11. colloquial	COL	_____	
	LOQU	_____	_____
12. convert	CON	_____	
	VERT	_____	_____
13. credible	CRED	_____	

		MEANING OF ROOT	MEANING OF WORD
14. emissary	E	_____	
	MISS	_____	_____
15. equate	EQU	_____	_____
16. euphony	EU	_____	
	PHON	_____	_____
17. evoke	E	_____	
	VOC	_____	_____
18. expedient	EX	_____	
	PED	_____	_____
19. fidelity	FID	_____	_____ _____
20. genealogy	GEN	_____	
	-LOGY	_____	_____
21. malady	MAL	_____	_____
22. monogram	MONO	_____	
	GRAM	_____	_____
23. pandemic	PAN	_____	
	DEM	_____	_____
24. philanthropy	PHIL	_____	
	ANTHROP	_____	_____
25. phobia	PHOB	_____	_____
26. preposterous	PRE	_____	
	POST	_____	_____
27. prologue	PRO	_____	
	LOG	_____	_____
28. prospectus	PRO	_____	
	SPECT	_____	_____

		MEANING OF ROOT	MEANING OF WORD
29. retort	RE	_____	
	TORT	_____	_____
30. subside	SUB	_____	
	SID	_____	_____
31. superannuated	SUPER	_____	
	ANN	_____	_____
32. telepathy	TELE	_____	
	PATH	_____	_____
33. trivia	TRI	_____	
	VIA	_____	_____
34. verify	VER	_____	_____

COMPREHENSIVE TEST C The words in these sentences contain all the roots you have studied. Put a C in front of each sentence in which all words are used correctly. No answers are provided at the back of the book for this test.

_____ 1. He felt apathetic about his job, not caring whether he kept it or not.

_____ 2. The bald eagle, an amphibian, is the national bird of the United States.

_____ 3. A triennial convention is held every three years.

_____ 4. My mother plants perennials so she won't have to buy new plants each year.

_____ 5. The anterior legs of an animal are those at the front.

_____ 6. Gorillas and zebras are anthropoids.

_____ 7. Our contestant found that he faced a powerful antagonist.

_____ 8. Taking no interest in her work, she performed it like an automaton.

_____ 9. The monarch had a benign attitude toward his subjects, always thinking of their welfare.

_____ 10. The new highway bisects the city.

_____ 11. The biopsy proved that the growth was benign.

_____ 12. Her chronic cough has lasted for years.

_____ 13. She takes forever to say anything because she uses so many circumlocutions.

_____ 14. A coherent paper is well organized and sticks to the point.

_____ 15. A four-year-old is amazingly credulous and will believe anything you say.

_____ 16. Television was the precursor of movies.

_____ 17. An endemic plant is one that is widespread over the entire earth.

_____ 18. A jurisdiction is a sentence given by a judge to someone who is guilty.

_____ 19. He was disconcerted by the noise in the back of the auditorium.

_____ 20. Becoming upset over the criticism, he lost his usual equanimity.

_____ 21. After I lost that tennis match, I was in a state of euphoria.

_____ 22. Receiving that scholarship expedited my getting through college.

_____ 23. She accused him of fidelity and threatened to get a divorce.

_____ 24. He has always been diffident and dreads speaking in public.

_____ 25. Praise often engenders greater loyalty in employees.

_____ 26. By using many details, he gave a graphic picture of the storm.

_____ 27. The play began with a monologue between the two main characters.

_____ 28. Studying word roots in this book has given me an interest in etymology.

_____ 29. Her loquacious phone calls show up on my phone bill.

_____ 30. I missed class because I was really ill; I wasn't malingering.

_____ 31. The odometer indicated that my blood pressure was above normal.

_____ 32. A missive is a weapon.

_____ 33. Monogamy is the belief that there is only one God.

_____ 34. The lecturer's presentation was simply an amorphous collection of unrelated stories.

_____ 35. Do you expect the encounter group to be a panacea for all your problems?

_____ 36. She felt extreme antipathy for her sister and liked to spend as much time with her as she could.

_____ 37. Improving my vocabulary has impeded my ability to read with understanding.

_____ 38. He's a born philanthropist, criticizing everyone and in general hating people.

_____ 39. Because of her claustrophobia, she refused to enter the cave.

_____ 40. Polyphonic means having two or more melodies combined.

_____ 41. Because I want to leave a record for posterity, I'm writing our family history.

_____ 42. Being given a month's vacation was unprecedented; no one had ever been given that long a vacation before.

_____ 43. As a proponent of conservation, he has been making speeches advocating paper recycling.

_____ 44. Now that she has established new habits, she's not likely to revert to the old ones.

_____ 45. A new employee needs to be circumspect about offering suggestions.

_____ 46. Abraham Lincoln ascribed his success to his mother.

_____ 47. Because I have a sedentary job, I try to walk a mile every evening.

_____ 48. When I was in France, I didn't find my inability to speak French an insuperable barrier.

_____ 49. Symbiosis is the living together of two different organisms in what is usually a mutually beneficial relationship.

_____ 50. Telepathy is the sending of messages by Morse code.

_____ 51. The tortuous mountain road was nothing but twists and turns.

_____ 52. He went sailing on the lake in his subterfuge.

_____ 53. I'd never question her veracity because I've known her for years and have always found her truthful.

Answers

p. 9 PRELIMINARY TEST

1. B	6. B	11. D	16. C	21. B	26. A
2. D	7. C	12. A	17. D	22. C	27. D
3. A	8. A	13. A	18. B	23. D	
4. A	9. B	14. B	19. A	24. B	
5. D	10. C	15. D	20. C	25. C	

p. 13 EXERCISE 1

1. anecdotes
2. asymmetrical
3. anonymous
4. anomaly
5. anarchy
6. agnostic
7. atheist
8. amoral
9. anesthetics
10. anemia
11. atypical

p. 15 EXERCISE 1

1. A
2. C
3. B
4. F
5. E
6. D

EXERCISE 2

1. ambiguous
2. ambivalent
3. ambivalence
4. ambience
5. ambiguity
6. amphibians
7. ambidextrous
8. amphitheater

p. 17 EXERCISE 1

1. centennial
2. millennium
3. annals
4. annuity
5. anniversary
6. semiannual or biannual
7. biennial
8. perennial
9. superannuated

EXERCISE 2 REVIEW

1. ambience
2. ambiguity
3. atypical
4. ambivalent
5. anomaly
6. amphibian
7. amphibians

p. 19 EXERCISE 1

1. antiquated
2. antediluvian
3. anterior
4. antebellum
5. antiquarian
6. antiquity
7. antedate
8. ante
9. antecedent
10. anticipated

p. 21 EXERCISE 1

1. anthropomorphic
2. anthropologist
3. misanthrope
4. anthropology
5. anthropoid
6. philanthropist

p. 23 EXERCISE 1

1. anticlimax
2. antagonist
3. antithesis
4. antibiotics
5. antidote
6. Antarctica
7. antiseptics

p. 25 EXERCISE 1

1. autocratic
2. automaton
3. autocrat
4. autocracy
5. autonomic
6. autonomous
7. automatic

EXERCISE 2 REVIEW
All sentences are correct except 2, 8, 9, 11, 15.

p. 27 EXERCISE 1

1. benediction
2. benefactor
3. beneficence
4. benign
5. benevolent
6. beneficiary
7. benevolence or beneficence
8. beneficial

EXERCISE 2 REVIEW
All sentences are correct except 1.
1. anthropoids

p. 29 EXERCISE 1

1. bilateral
2. bipartisan
3. bicameral
4. bivalve
5. bisect
6. biceps
7. binoculars
8. bicentennial
9. bilingual
10. bigamy
11. bicuspid
12. bipeds

p. 31 EXERCISE 1
All sentences are correct except 5, 6, 13.
5. bilingual
6. biped
13. biofeedback

p. 33 EXERCISE 1

1. chronological
2. anachronism
3. synchronize
4. chronometer
5. chronic

EXERCISE 2 REVIEW

1. chronicle
2. anarchy
3. bicameral
4. antique
5. antebellum
6. anachronism
7. misanthropic
8. biofeedback
9. autonomous

p. 35 EXERCISE 1

1. circumlocution
2. circumvent
3. circumspect
4. circumscribe
5. circuitous
6. circumnavigated

EXERCISE 2 REVIEW
All sentences are correct except 7, 8.

EXERCISE 3
We'll be glad to repair your TV set free of charge.

p. 38 EXERCISE 1

1. commensurate
2. condone
3. correlate
4. consummate
5. compunction
6. commodious
7. commiserate
8. collusion
9. consensus
10. collaborate or cooperate
11. congenital
12. condominium
13. coherent
14. convene
15. convivial

p. 41 EXERCISE 1

1. B
2. C
3. D
4. E
5. A
6. F

EXERCISE 2

1. credible
2. incredulity
3. credence
4. miscreant
5. incredulous
6. credulity
7. credulous
8. incredible
9. credibility
10. credentials

p. 43 EXERCISE 1

1. B
2. F
3. D
4. A
5. C
6. E

EXERCISE 2

1. cursory
2. concurrent
3. recurrent
4. concur
5. cursive
6. recourse
7. precursor
8. concourse
9. discourses
10. recur

p. 45 EXERCISE 1

1. endemic
2. demagogue
3. epidemic
4. pandemic
5. Demographic
6. demagoguery

p. 47 EXERCISE 1

1. jurisdiction
2. diction
3. dictatorial
4. abdicated
5. edict
6. dictum
7. valedictorian
8. addicted

EXERCISE 2 REVIEW

1. anthropology
2. anachronism
3. beneficiary
4. biped
5. amoral
6. bigamy

p. 49 EXERCISE 1

1. dissuade
2. disarray
3. disburse
4. disseminate
5. discomfited or disconcerted
6. dismantled
7. disparity
8. disparate or diverse
9. discordant

p. 51 EXERCISE 1

1. equate
2. equivocated
3. equity
4. equanimity
5. equilibrium
6. equable
7. equinox
8. equilateral
9. equivocal
10. equitable

EXERCISE 2 REVIEW

All answers are correct except 2, 5, 6, 7, 11, 17, 22, 26, 30, 32

p. 54 EXERCISE 1

1. eulogized
2. euphonious
3. eulogy
4. euphemism
5. euphoria
6. euphony
7. euthanasia

EXERCISE 2 REVIEW

All sentences are correct except 3, 11.
3. antidote
11. collision

p. 57 EXERCISE 1

1. enervating
2. efface
3. exonerate
4. expurgated
5. ebullient
6. emolument
7. expatiated
8. excoriated

p. 59 EXERCISE 1

1. bona fide
2. diffident
3. perfidious
4. infidel
5. fidelity
6. confidant

p. 61 EXERCISE 1

1. genesis
2. genealogy
3. engenders
4. progenitor
5. genre
6. progeny
7. ingenuous

p. 63 EXERCISE 1

1. graphic
2. monogram
3. choreography
4. topography
5. cardiogram
6. graffiti
7. monograph
8. epigram

p. 64 EXERCISE 1

1. epilogue
2. monologue
3. prologue
4. analogy
5. dialogue
6. analogous

p. 65 EXERCISE 2 REVIEW

All sentences are correct except 2, 5, 12, 14.
2. anecdotes
5. dialogue
12. ingenious
14. philanthropist

p. 67 EXERCISE 1

1. psychology
2. meteorology
3. etymology
4. geology
5. archeology
6. entomology
7. ornithology
8. embryology
9. ecology

p. 69 EXERCISE 1

1. loquacious
2. colloquial
3. grandiloquent
4. soliloquy
5. ventriloquist
6. colloquium

EXERCISE 2 REVIEW

All sentences are correct except 3, 8, 12.

p. 71 EXERCISE 1

1. malinger
2. malady
3. malcontent
4. malicious
5. malignant
6. malign
7. malice
8. malediction
9. malfeasance
10. malevolent
11. malaise
12. maladroit
13. malapropisms

p. 72 EXERCISE 3 REVIEW

All sentences are correct except 6.
6. infidelity

p. 75 EXERCISE 1

1. perimeter
2. barometer
3. odometer
4. kilometer
5. metronome
6. pedometer
7. symmetrical
8. tachometer

EXERCISE 2 REVIEW

1. disproportionate
2. expatiated
3. cursory
4. progenitors

p. 79 EXERCISE 1

1. monosyllable
2. Monotheism
3. monotone
4. monogamy
5. monolithic
6. monoliths

EXERCISE 2 REVIEW

All sentences are correct except 7, 10, 12.

p. 80 EXERCISE 1

1. mesomorphic
2. morphology
3. Morphine
4. endomorphic
5. amorphous
6. ectomorphic
7. metamorphosis

EXERCISE 2 REVIEW

All sentences are correct except 2, 5.
2. benediction
5. malevolent

EXERCISE 3 REVIEW

1. antiquarian
2. anthropologist
3. atheist
4. philanthropist
5. dissident

p. 83 EXERCISE 1

1. pandemonium
2. panacea
3. pantheism
4. panorama
5. Pantomime
6. panoply
7. pantheon
8. panchromatic

EXERCISE 2 REVIEW

All sentences are correct except 2, 4, 6.

p. 85 EXERCISE 1

1. apathetic
2. empathy
3. psychopathic
4. antipathy
5. pathological
6. pathos
7. apathetic

EXERCISE 2 REVIEW

1. D
2. E
3. A
4. C
5. F
6. B

p. 87 EXERCISE 1

1. expedite
2. expedient
3. impede
4. pedigree
5. impediment

EXERCISE 2 REVIEW

1. equable
2. ingenious
3. ebullient
4. disparity
5. around
6. euphonious

p. 89 EXERCISE 1

1. B	3. F	5. D
2. E	4. C	6. A

EXERCISE 2 REVIEW

1. morphology	6. antipathy	11. philatelist
2. etymology	7. pantomime	12. pantheon
3. monolithic	8. expedite	13. equitable
4. calligraphy	9. perfidious	14. panchromatic
5. malfeasance	10. analogy	

p. 90 EXERCISE 1

1. photophobia	4. claustrophobia	7. technophobia
2. phobic	5. hydrophobia	8. phobia
3. xenophobia	6. acrophobia	

p. 93 EXERCISE 1

1. cacophony	3. saxophone	5. phonetics
2. polyphonic	4. megaphone	

EXERCISE 2 REVIEW

All sentences are correct except 4, 8.

4. claustrophobia	8. missiles

p. 95 EXERCISE 1

1. posthumously	4. posterior	7. postmortem
2. posterity	5. postlude	
3. preposterous	6. Postimpressionists	

EXERCISE 2 REVIEW

1. emolument	6. xenophobia	11. postlude
2. excoriate	7. dissidents	12. odometer
3. disparate	8. monocle	13. pathology
4. equivocate	9. ambience	
5. disconcerted	10. biannual	

p. 97 EXERCISE 1

1. precipitated	5. unprecedented	9. precludes
2. precocious	6. preeminent	10. prerequisite
3. precedent	7. preponderant	
4. predilection	8. presage	

p. 99 EXERCISE 1

1. prospectus	4. protuberant	7. promontory
2. proclivity or propensity	5. procrastinate	8. provident
3. proponent	6. profusion	9. profuse

p. 101 EXERCISE 1

1. recession	4. resilience	7. remiss
2. recalcitrant	5. remission	8. recant
3. revert	6. recluse	

p. 102 EXERCISE 2 REVIEW

All sentences are correct except 4, 8.

4. monogram	8. astronomy

p. 105 EXERCISE 1

1. ascribe
2. nondescript
3. transcribe
4. conscription
5. subscribe
6. proscribed

EXERCISE 2 REVIEW
All sentences are correct except 5, 6, 10, 12, 13, 14.

p. 107 EXERCISE 1

1. sedentary
2. assiduous
3. subsidy
4. insidious
5. subside
6. superseded
7. obsession
8. subsidiary
9. obsessed
10. assess
11. assessor

p. 109 EXERCISE 1

1. auspicious
2. perspective
3. retrospect
4. introspection
5. despicable
6. perspicacious
7. specious
8. spectrum
9. specter
10. speculate

p. 111 EXERCISE 1

1. submerged
2. subjected
3. subsistence
4. subversive
5. subterfuge
6. subservient
7. subjugate
8. subliminal
9. subsumed
10. subpoena
11. subterranean
12. sub rosa

p. 113 EXERCISE 1

1. supersonic
2. superfluous
3. superimpose
4. insuperable
5. supercilious

p. 115 EXERCISE 1

1. synthesis
2. symposium
3. Synthetic
4. syndrome
5. synod
6. syntax
7. syllogism
8. synergistic
9. symbol

p. 119 EXERCISE 1

1. extort
2. retort
3. contortionist
4. distort
5. tortuous
6. torturous
7. tort

EXERCISE 2 REVIEW
All sentences are correct except 1, 7, 9, 10.

p. 121 EXERCISE 1

1. Trinity
2. tripod or trivet
3. trident
4. trilogy
5. trilingual
6. triennial
7. tripartite or trilateral

EXERCISE 2 REVIEW
All sentences are correct except 3, 6, 10, 11.

p. 122 EXERCISE 1

1. veritable
2. veracity
3. verify
4. verification
5. veracious
6. verifiable
7. verities

p. 123 EXERCISE 2 REVIEW

1. insidious
2. phobic
3. subversive
4. photophobia
5. ascribed

6. veracity
7. presage
8. obsessed
9. trilogy
10. trivet

11. triennial
12. promontory
13. monotheism
14. graphite
15. tripartite

p. 125 EXERCISE 1

1. adversary
2. Obverse
3. inadvertent
4. introvert

5. averse
6. perverse
7. adversity
8. adverse

9. averted
10. versatile
11. aversion

p. 127 EXERCISE 3 REVIEW

1. prospect   a looking forward
2. chronic   continuing for a long time
3. concurred   agreed
4. edicts   official decrees
5. propensity   natural inclination
6. aversion   extreme dislike
7. spectrum   broad range
8. panacea   remedy for all ills
9. prologue   introductory event
10. posterity   future generations
11. circumvent   prevent
12. unprecedented   never having happened before

p. 128 EXERCISE 1 REVIEW

All sentences are correct except 2, 6, 10, 15, 23.

p. 131 EXERCISE 1

1. irrevocable
2. evoke
3. invoked
4. avocation

5. vociferous
6. evocative
7. invocation
8. convocation

9. revoked
10. vocation

EXERCISE 2 REVIEW

All answers are correct except 3, 12.
3. bilateral   12. acrophobia

p. 132 COMPREHENSIVE TEST A

1. B	6. C	11. C	16. D	21. C	26. C
2. C	7. A	12. A	17. D	22. D	27. C
3. D	8. D	13. C	18. B	23. C	
4. C	9. A	14. D	19. A	24. B	
5. B	10. D	15. C	20. D	25. A	

p. 134 COMPREHENSIVE TEST B

1. AMPHI both, BIO life.   an animal that lives both in water and on land; a plane that can land on water or on land
2. ANTE before.   to occur before something else
3. ANTHROP human, MORPH form.   thought of as having human form or characteristics
4. ANTI against, BIO life.   a substance used against living microorganisms
5. A not, SYM together, METR to measure.   not having both sides equal
6. AUTO self, GRAPH to write.   one's signature

7. BENE good, DICT to speak.   a blessing
8. BI two, ENN year.   occurring every two years
9. CHRON time, METER measure.   an instrument for measuring time, especially in navigation
10. CIRCUM around, SCRIB to write.   to confine
11. COL together, LOQU to speak.   informal
12. CON together, VERT to turn.   to cause to turn from one belief to another
13. CRED to believe.   believable
14. E out, MISS to send.   a person sent out on a specific mission
15. EQU equal.   to represent as equal
16. EU good, PHON sound.   pleasing sounds
17. E out, VOC to call.   to call forth, as memories or feelings
18. EX out, PED foot.   *lit.* foot out of an entanglement; useful in getting a desired result
19. FID faith.   faithfulness
20. GEN race, -LOGY study of.   the study of family descent
21. MAL bad.   a disease
22. MONO one, GRAM to write.   letters entwined into one design
23. PAN all, DEM people.   widespread
24. PHIL love, ANTHROP human.   helping humanity with charitable donations
25. PHOB fear.   an excessive or illogical fear
26. PRE before, POST after.   absurd
27. PRO before, LOG speech.   a speech before a play; an introductory event
28. PRO forward, SPECT to look.   a summary of a proposed venture
29. RE back, TORT to twist.   a reply to an insult or criticism
30. SUB under, SID to sit.   to settle down
31. SUPER above, ANN year.   retired because of age
32. TELE far, PATH feeling.   the supposed communication of two people far apart
33. TRI three, VIA way.   unimportant matters
34. VER true.   to prove something is true

Word Index